Stories Behind The Art

Biographies

Wayne Pascall

Stories Behind The Art -Biographies

Featured Art and Biographies of:

Steve Jobs
Albert Einstein
Maya Angelou
Mahatma Gandhi
Helen Keller
Florence Nightingale
Nelson Mandela
Jesus The Christ
Edward Deming
Martin Luther King Jr.
Chief Sitting Bull
Bob Marley
Marilyn Monroe
Ray Charles
The Woman at The Well

PREFACE

Stories Behind The Art

Biographies

By

Wayne Pascall

Here is a collection of my favorite pieces of portraits rendered in pencil, acrylic paint and oil paint. They represent artistic works I have produced over the past 18 years. I have selected the pieces below because they each represent a person or setting that was inspirational to me. I love doing portraits, sunsets, nature and still life. My favorite medium is pencil, acrylic paint, occasionally pen and ink and some oils.

My love for art started from a very small child. I remember drawing from an early age as early as 4 years old. My father had drawn a picture on the cover of my baby diary. I was always attempting to imitate his drawing and thus my skill developed all through High School, where it was further refined by art classes at Presentation College San Fernando. I love art! I see art as a powerful tool for communication, instruction, storytelling and is very therapeutic. When I compose both art and music, I escape into a magical world where time does not exist and all things are possible.

I hope that you find inspiration in lives of the people I have featured in these drawings and paintings. You can access more of my art at Fineartamerica.com where you can purchase pieces in various sizes from 10 inches to 48 inches in length, add a frame of your choice, printed on a material of your choice. You can even purchase my art as greeting cards and iPhone cases. Peace be unto you!

http://wayne-pascall.artistwebsites.com/

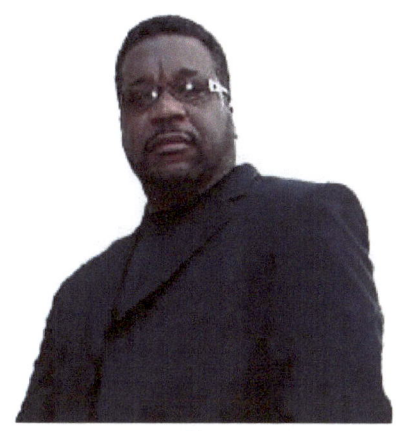

Steve Jobs
STEVE JOBS (1955-2011)

Steve Jobs the founder of Apple, brought us the Mac computer, iTunes, the iPod and iPad. As an artist, I have to thank Steve Jobs for creating such an innovative gadget like the iPad. It has made creating digital art pure joy. Here is one of Steve's inspirational quotes.

"Here's to the crazy ones, the misfits, the rebels, the troublemakers, the round pegs in the square holes... the ones who see things differently - they're not fond of rules... You can quote them, disagree with them, glorify or vilify them, but the only thing you can't do is ignore them because they change things... they push the human race forward, and while some may see them as the crazy ones, we see genius, because the ones who are crazy enough to think that they can change the world, are the ones who do." – **Steve Jobs**

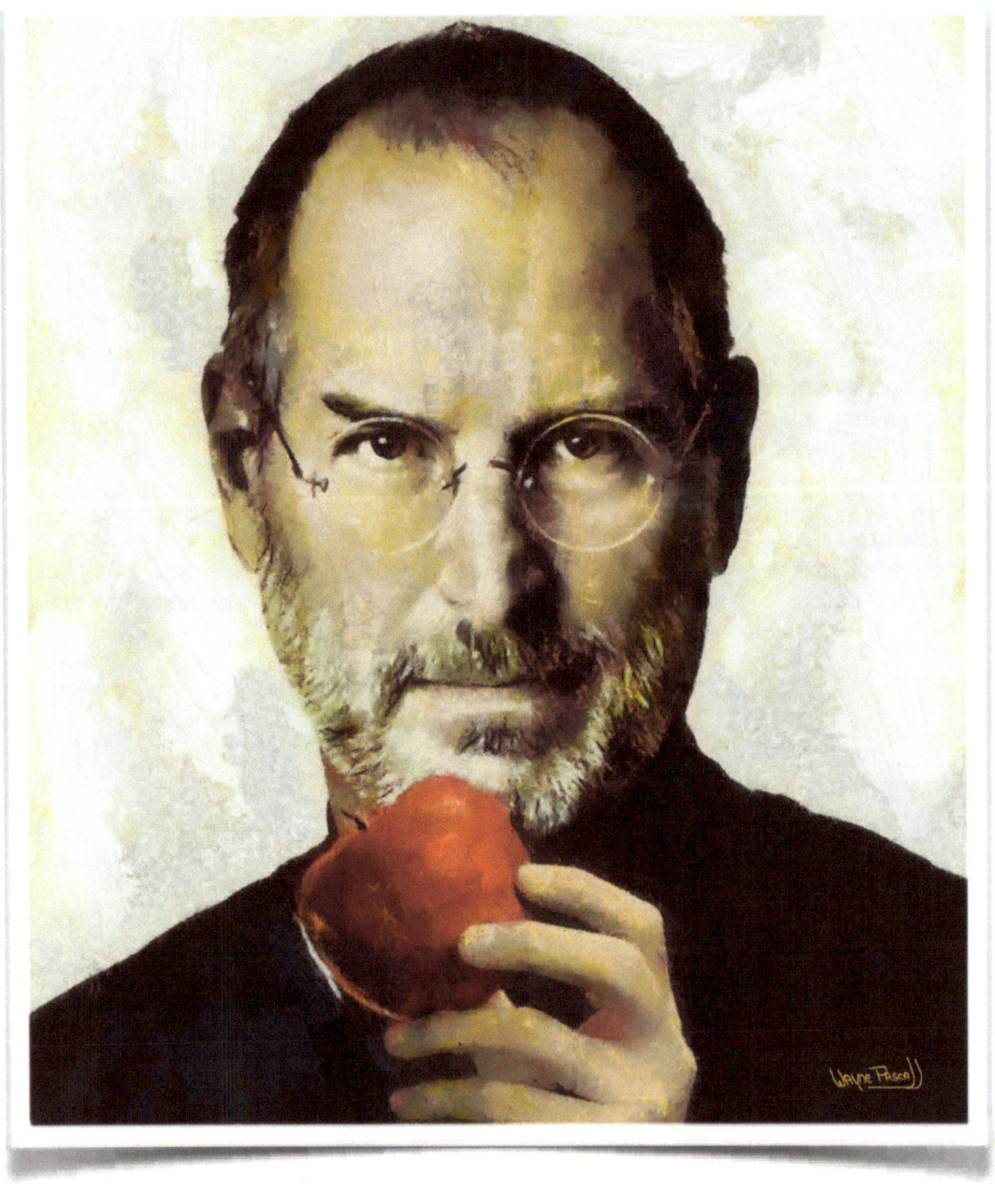

Steve Jobs

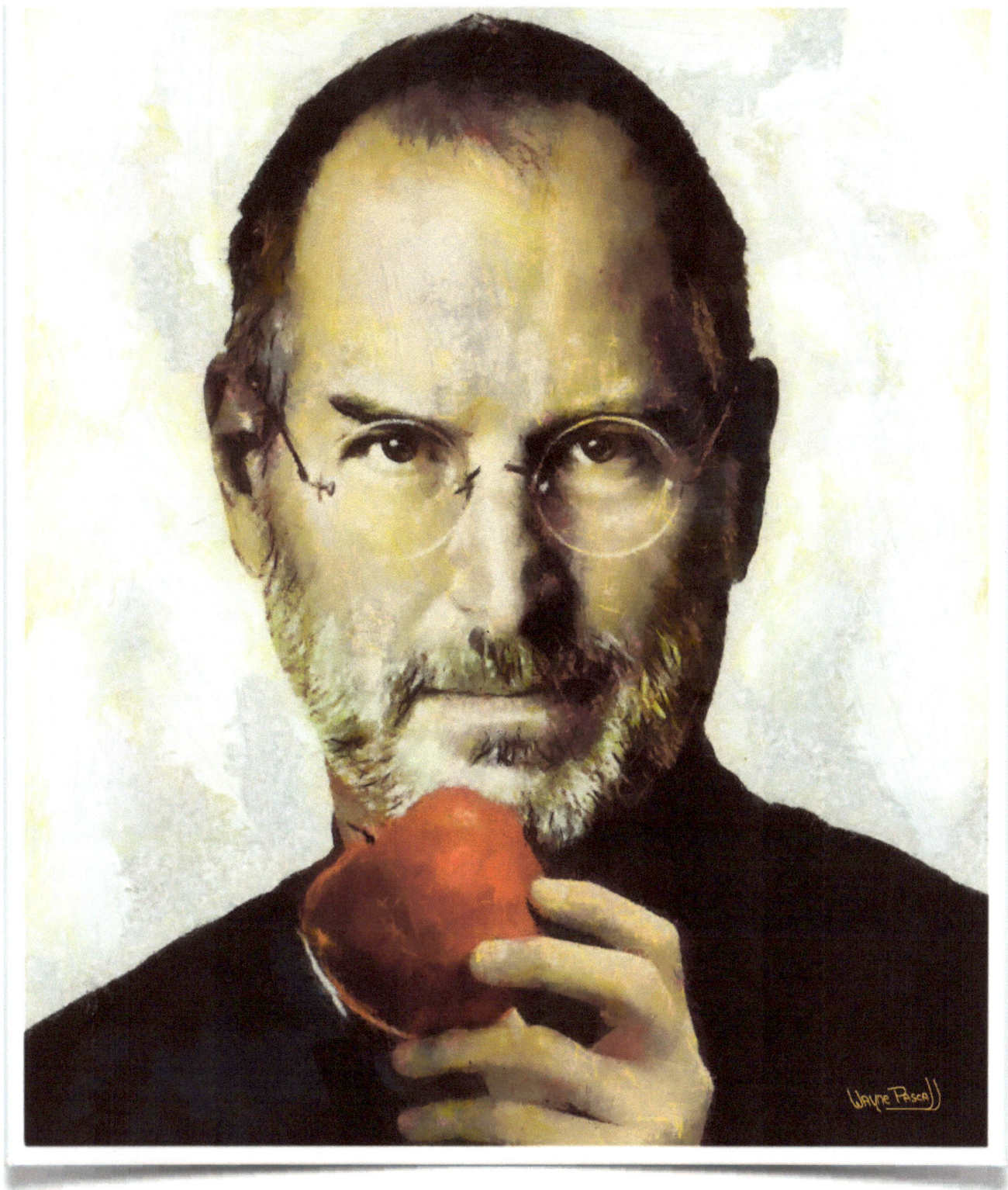

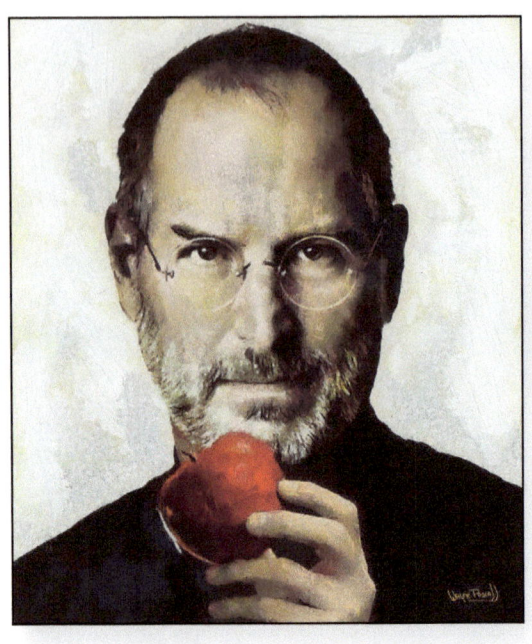

Steve Jobs

Wayne Pascall

http://wayne-pascall.artistwebsites.com/featured/steve-jobs-wayne-pascall.html

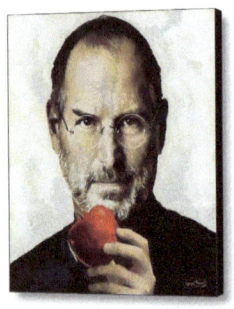

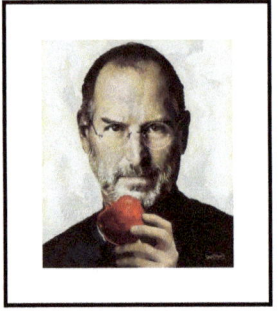

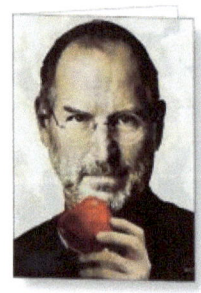

Stretched Canvases

Stretcher Bars: 1.50" x 1.50" or 0.625" x 0.625"
Wrap Style: Black, White, or Mirrored Image

6.88" x 8.00"	$62.04
8.75" x 10.00"	$79.96
10.50" x 12.00"	$98.86
12.25" x 14.00"	$112.17
13.88" x 16.00"	$117.17
17.50" x 20.00"	$154.47
20.88" x 24.00"	$182.77

Prices shown for 1.50" x 1.50" gallery-wrapped
prints with black sides.

Fine Art Prints

Choose From Thousands of Available
Frames, Mats, and Fine Art Papers

6.88" x 8.00"	$37.00
8.75" x 10.00"	$37.00
10.50" x 12.00"	$42.00
12.25" x 14.00"	$45.50
13.88" x 16.00"	$54.00
17.50" x 20.00"	$57.50
20.88" x 24.00"	$69.50

Prices shown for unframed / unmatted
prints on archival matte paper.

Greeting Cards

All Cards are 5" x 7" and Include
White Envelopes for Mailing and Gift Giving

Not Available

Scan With Smartphone
to Buy Online

Einstein

ALBERT EINSTEIN (1879-1955)

A German-born physicist and scientist best known for his mass–energy equivalence formula $E = mc^2$ – the world's most famous equation. In 1921, he received the Nobel prize for Physics. Amazingly, Einstein was deemed a slow learner in elementary school. Famous sayings by Einstein include:

"The important thing is not to stop questioning; curiosity has its own reason for existing. One cannot help but be in awe when contemplating the mysteries of eternity, of life, of the marvelous structure of reality. It is enough if one tries merely to comprehend a little of the mystery every day. The important thing is not to stop questioning; never lose a holy curiosity."

"I'm enough of an artist to draw freely on my imagination. Imagination is more important than knowledge. Knowledge is limited; imagination encircles the world." – Albert Einstein

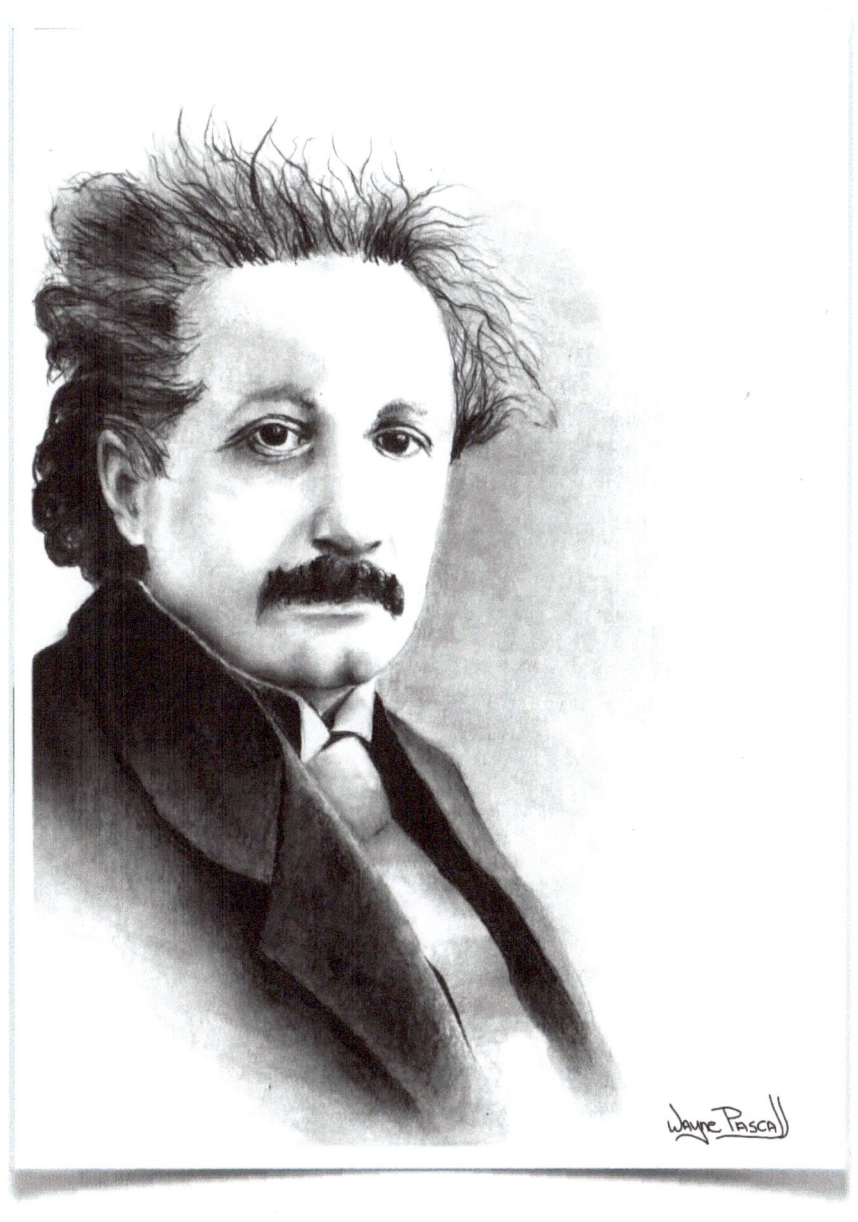

Einstein

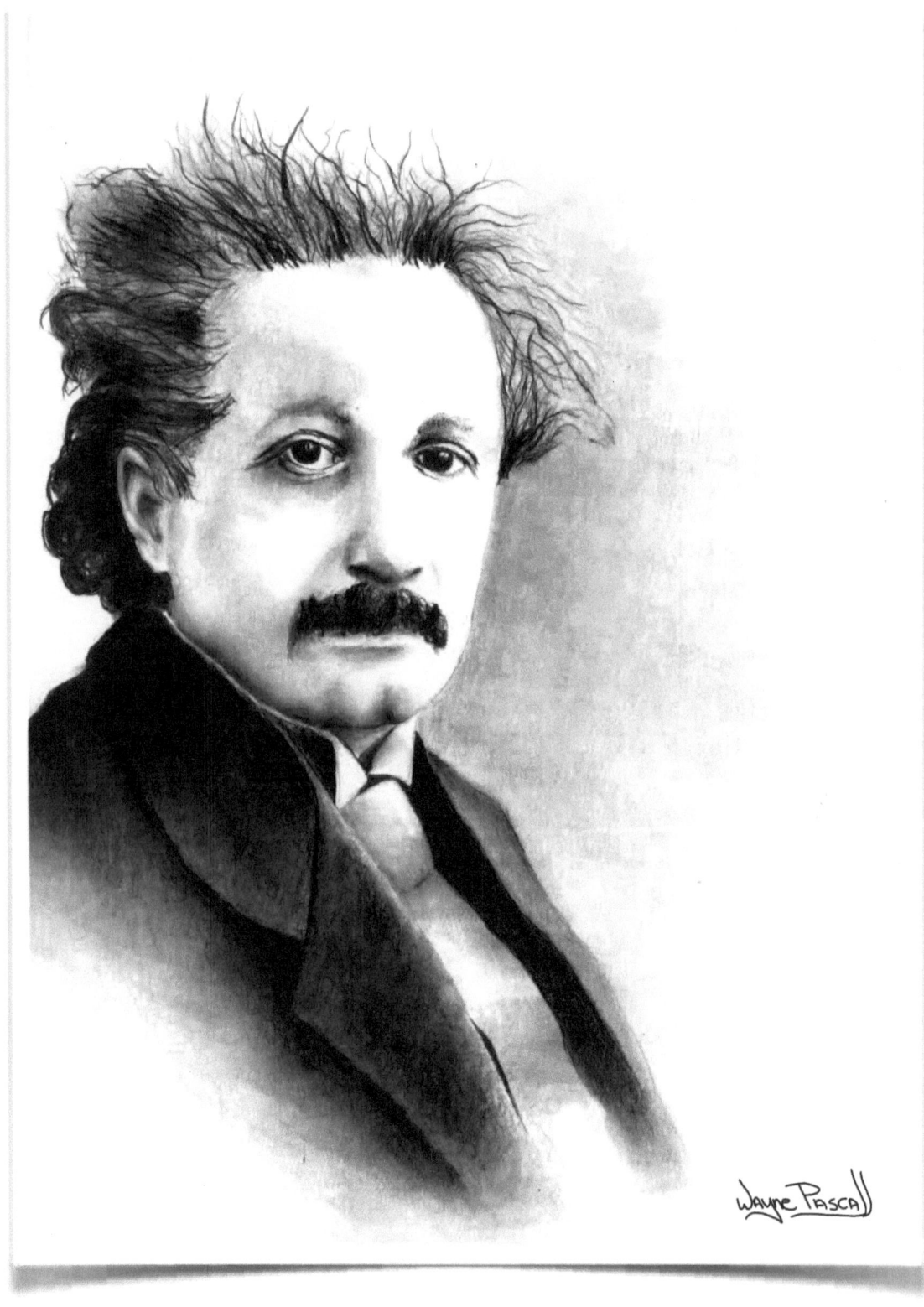

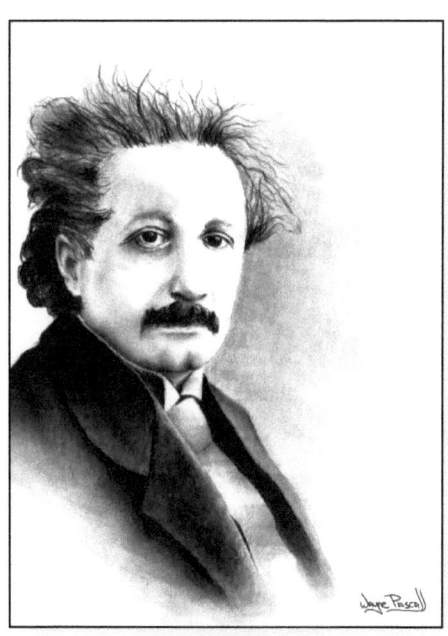

Einstein

Wayne Pascall

http://wayne-pascall.artistwebsites.com/featured/einstein-wayne-pascall.html

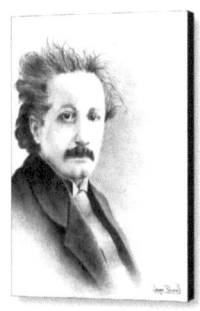 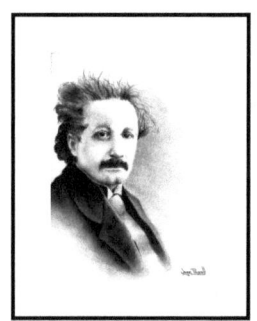 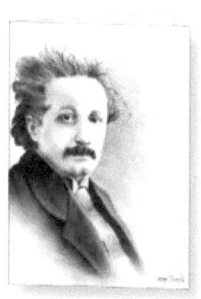

Stretched Canvases		Fine Art Prints		Greeting Cards	
Stretcher Bars: 1.50" x 1.50" or 0.625" x 0.625" Wrap Style: Black, White, or Mirrored Image		Choose From Thousands of Available Frames, Mats, and Fine Art Papers		All Cards are 5" x 7" and Include White Envelopes for Mailing and Gift Giving	
7.38" x 10.00"	$66.46	5.88" x 8.00"	$22.00	Single Card	$4.95 / Card
8.75" x 12.00"	$67.46	7.38" x 10.00"	$23.50	Pack of 10	$2.70 / Card
11.75" x 16.00"	$96.17	8.75" x 12.00"	$24.50	Pack of 25	$2.00 / Card
14.63" x 20.00"	$123.41	11.75" x 16.00"	$29.50		
17.63" x 24.00"	$149.26	14.63" x 20.00"	$38.50		
22.00" x 30.00"	$195.94	17.63" x 24.00"	$44.00		
26.38" x 36.00"	$239.15	22.00" x 30.00"	$60.00		
29.38" x 40.00"	$280.08	26.38" x 36.00"	$80.40		
35.25" x 48.00"	$355.75	29.38" x 40.00"	$93.45		
		35.25" x 48.00"	$122.40		

Prices shown for 1.50" x 1.50" gallery-wrapped prints with black sides.

Prices shown for unframed / unmatted prints on archival matte paper.

Scan With Smartphone to Buy Online

All prints and greeting cards are produced by Artist Websites (Artist Websites) and come with a 30-day money-back guarantee.

Orders may be placed online via credit card or PayPal. All orders ship within three business days from the AW production facility in North Carolina.

Maya Angelou
MAYA ANGELOU (1928-2014)

Dr. Maya Angelou also known as Marguerite Johnson was born on April 4, 1928, in St. Louis, Missouri. She has a colorful background as a renowned author, poet, memoirist, actress, educator, producer, dramatist, historian, filmmaker, civil rights activist and singer. She obviously reinvented herself having been a former prostitute.and performing menial jobs. She has lived an incredible life of various experiences, jobs, and relationships. Maya Angelou was known in her later years as a wonderful speaker and highly gifted author and poet.
Maya was a God-send and is hailed as one of the great voices of contemporary literature and as a remarkable Renaissance woman. She is one of the most well-known American authors and poets of this generation. She passed away in 2014.

"You can only become great at something you are willing to sacrifice for"
— Maya Angelou

"If you don't like something change it. If you can't change it, change you're attitude to it."
— Maya Angelou

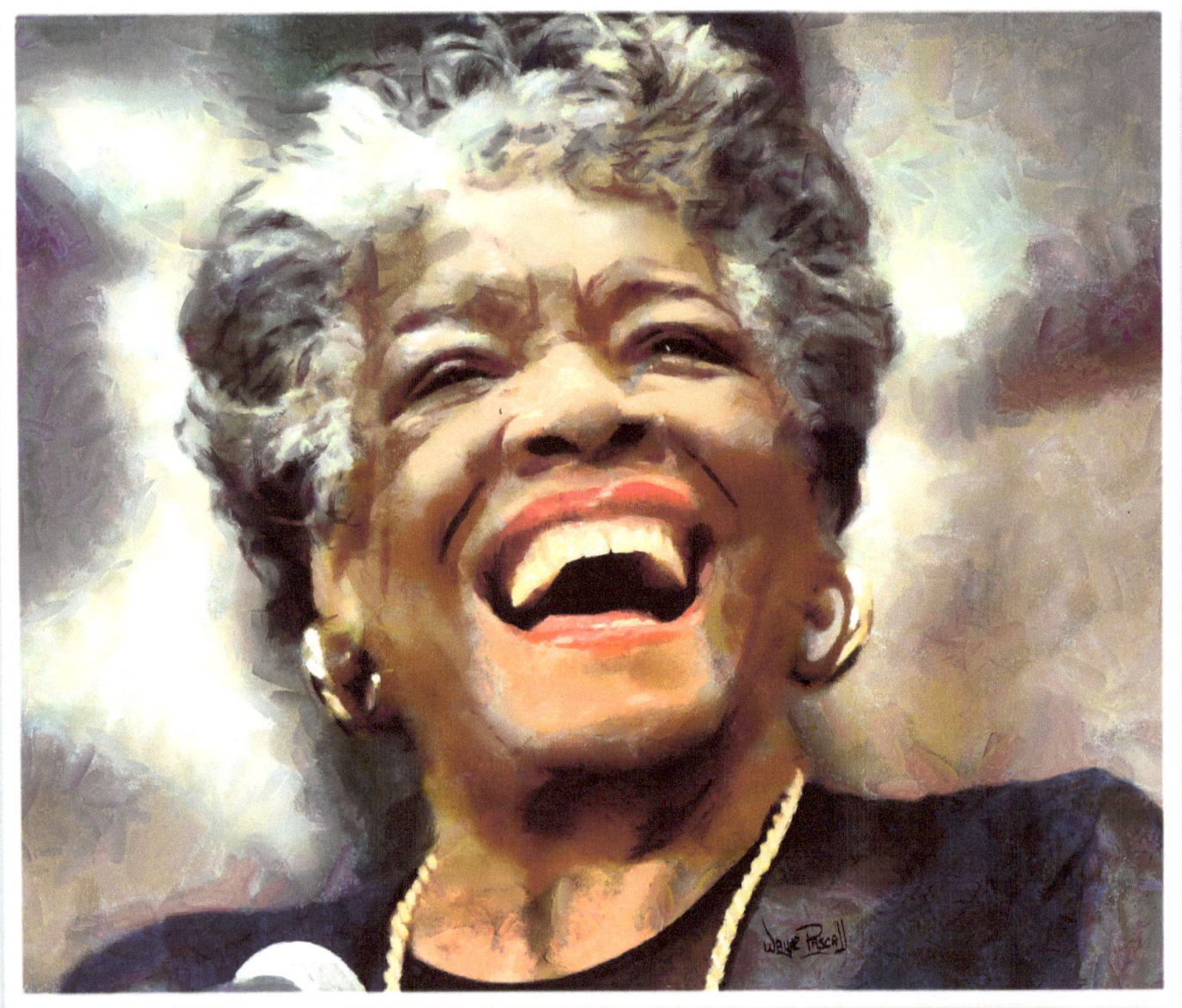

Maya Angelou

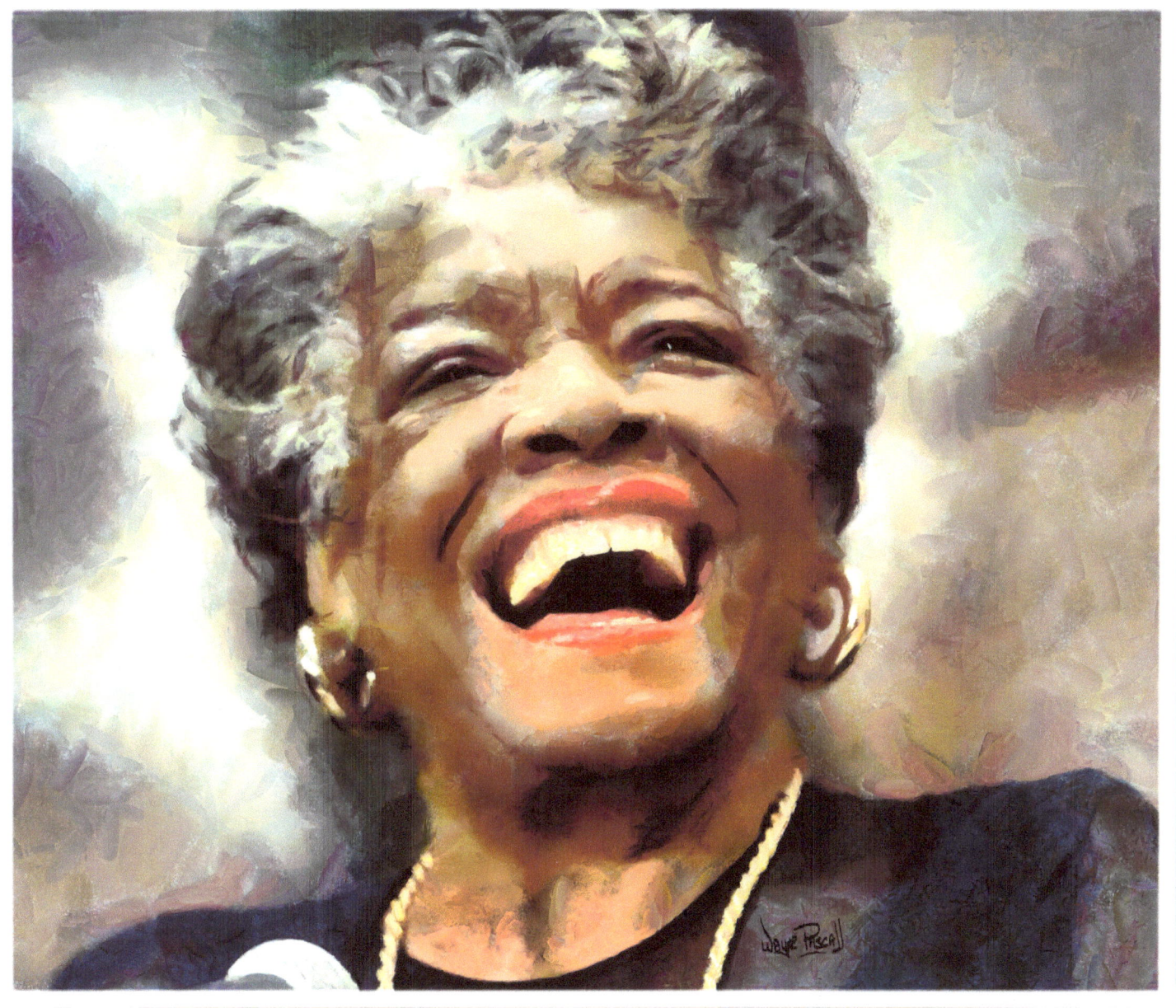

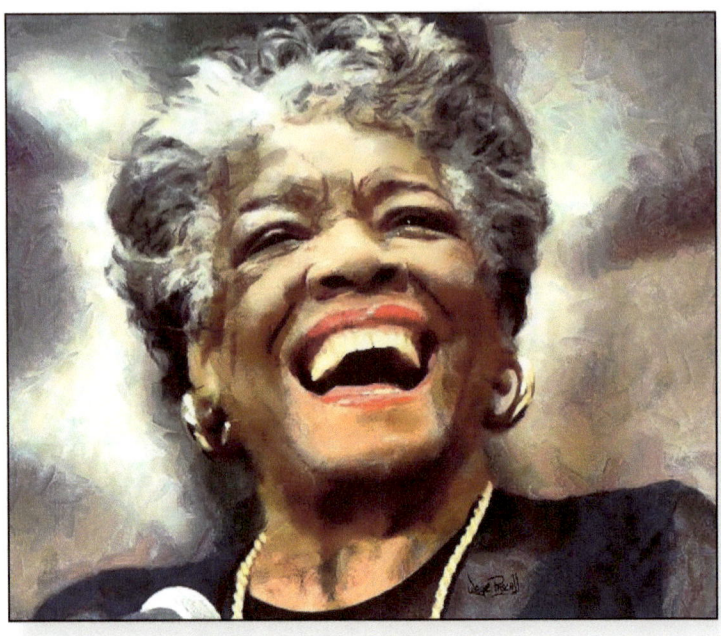

Maya Angelou
Wayne Pascall

http://wayne-pascall.artistwebsites.com/featured/maya-angelou-wayne-pascall.html

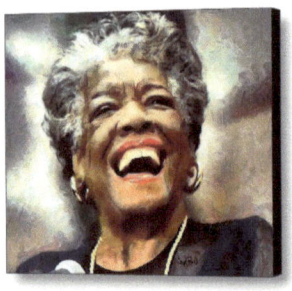
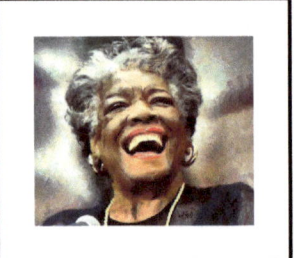
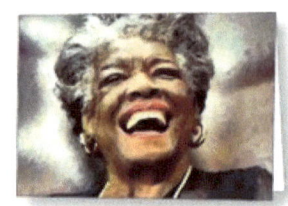

Stretched Canvases		Fine Art Prints		Greeting Cards	
Stretcher Bars: 1.50" x 1.50" or 0.625" x 0.625" Wrap Style: Black, White, or Mirrored Image		Choose From Thousands of Available Frames, Mats, and Fine Art Papers		All Cards are 5" x 7" and Include White Envelopes for Mailing and Gift Giving	
8.00" x 6.63"	$52.04	8.00" x 6.63"	$27.00	Single Card	$4.45 / Card
10.00" x 8.25"	$74.96	10.00" x 8.25"	$32.00	Pack of 10	$2.30 / Card
12.00" x 9.88"	$98.86	12.00" x 9.88"	$42.00	Pack of 25	$1.60 / Card
14.00" x 11.63"	$108.86	14.00" x 11.63"	$55.50		
16.00" x 13.25"	$137.17	16.00" x 13.25"	$70.50		
20.00" x 16.63"	$217.41	20.00" x 16.63"	$132.50		
24.00" x 19.88"	$307.77	24.00" x 19.88"	$194.50		
30.00" x 24.88"	$406.62	30.00" x 24.88"	$263.50		
36.00" x 29.88"	$512.62	36.00" x 29.88"	$337.75		
40.00" x 33.25"	$606.09	40.00" x 33.25"	$408.15		

Prices shown for 1.50" x 1.50" gallery-wrapped prints with black sides.

Prices shown for unframed / unmatted prints on archival matte paper.

Scan With Smartphone
to Buy Online

Mahatma Gandhi

MAHATMA GANDHI (1869-1948)

Mahatma Gandhi got independence for India through truth and non-violence. Mahatma Gandhi was born in 1869 and he remained a devout Hindu throughout his lifetime. Mahatma Gandhi was known as an international symbol for a free India. Mahatma Gandhi became a leader of the Indian community and over the years developed a political movement based on the methods of non-violent civil disobedience, which he called "satyagraha". Here are some famous sayings by Gandhi:

"The weak can never forgive. Forgiveness is the attribute of the strong."

"Live as if you were to die tomorrow. Learn as if you were to live forever."

"An error does not become truth by reason of multiplied propagation, nor does truth become error because nobody sees it." — *Mahatma Gandhi*

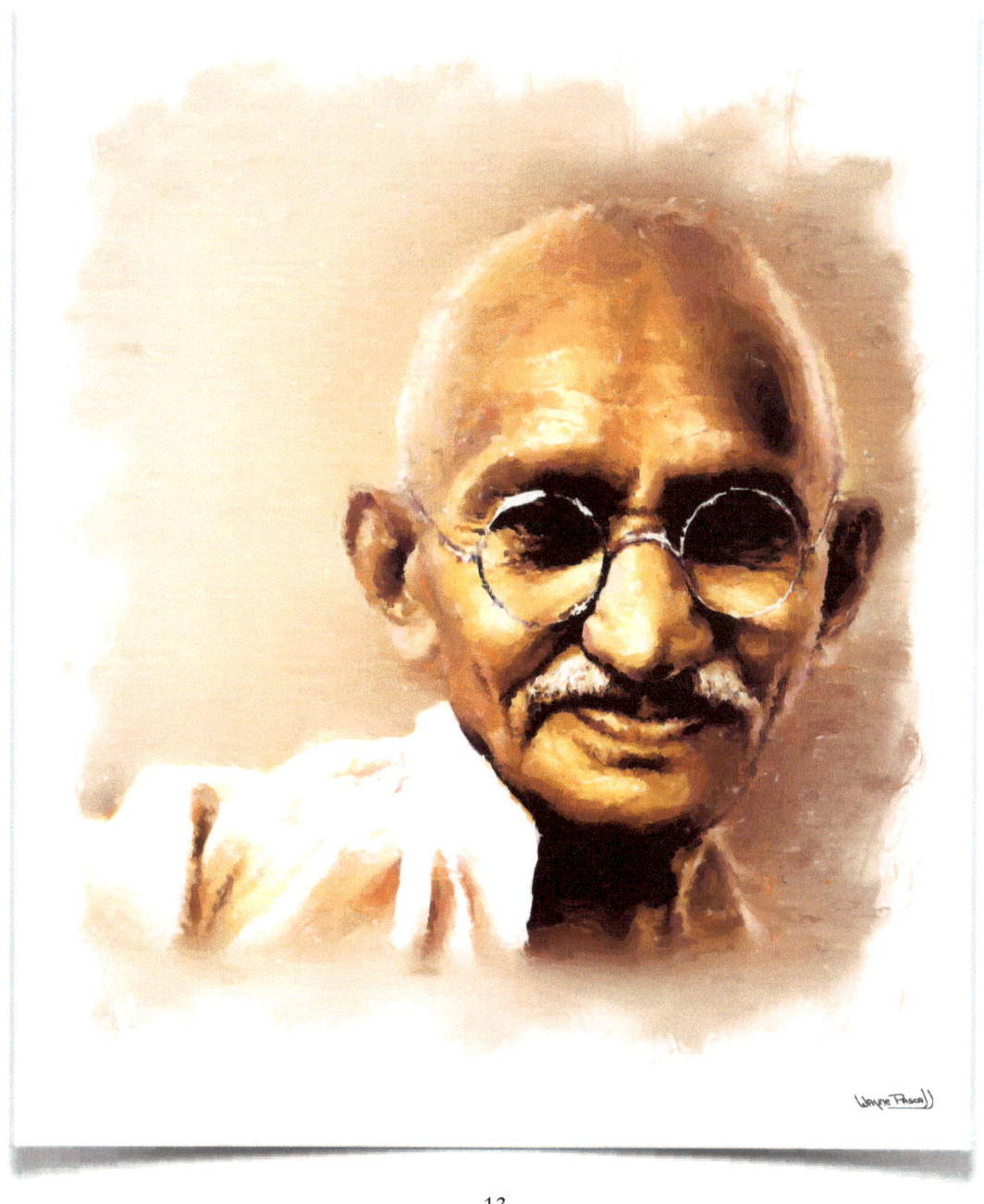

Mahatma Gandhi

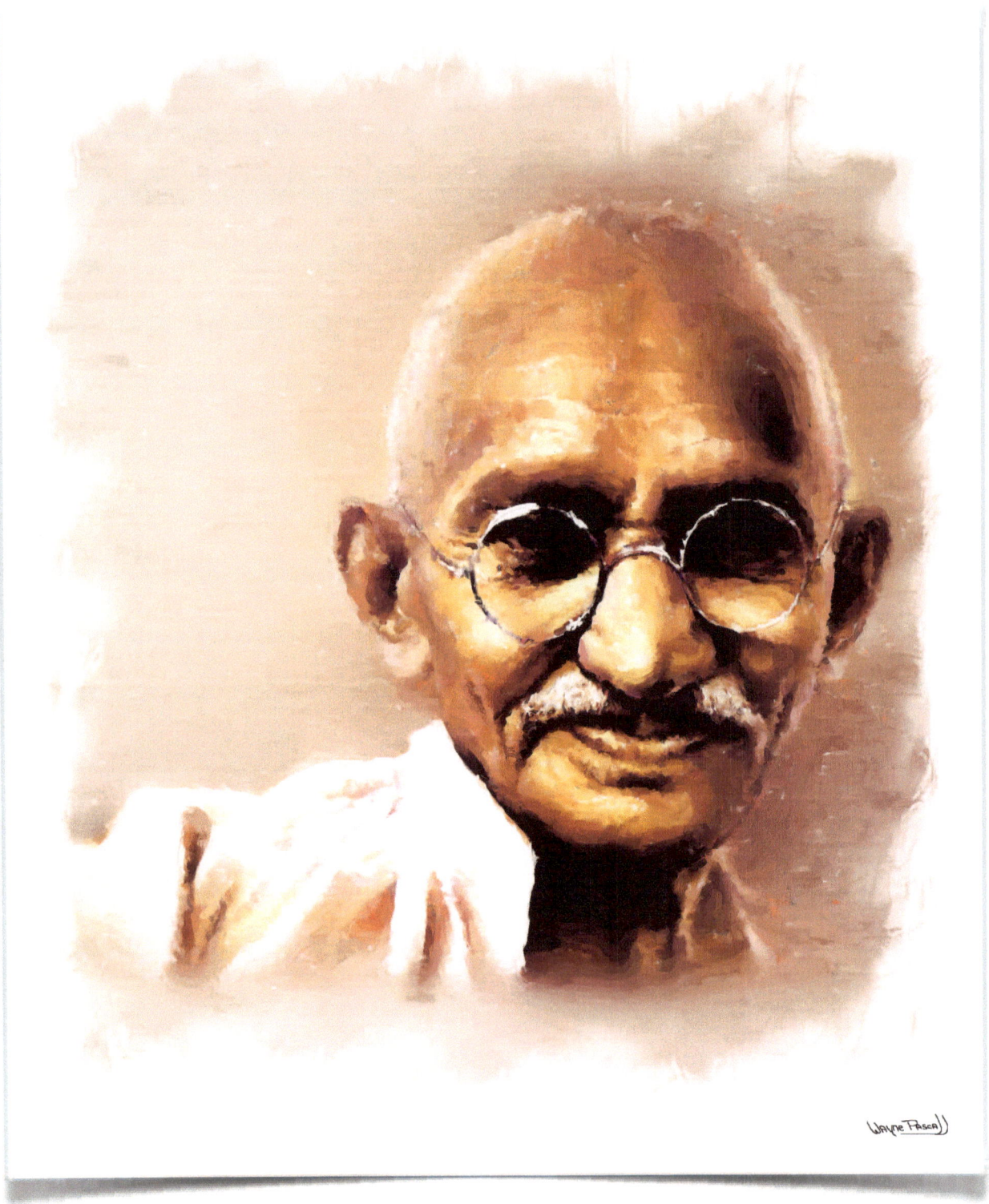

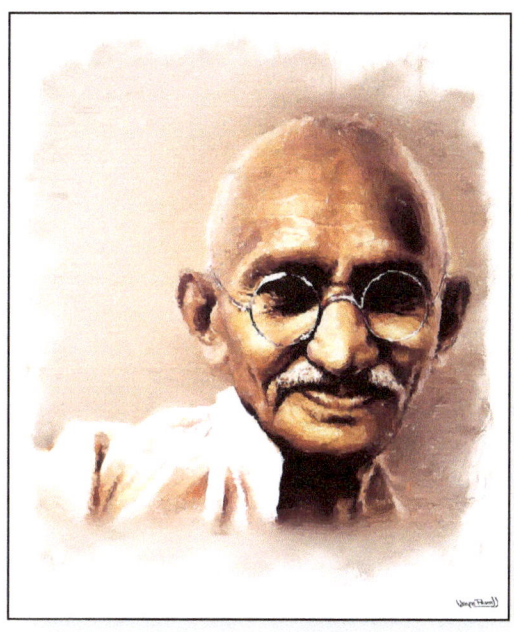

Gandhi in Color
Wayne Pascall

http://wayne-pascall.artistwebsites.com/featured/gandhi-in-color-wayne-pascall.html

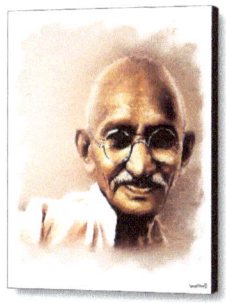 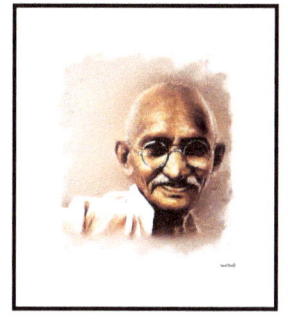 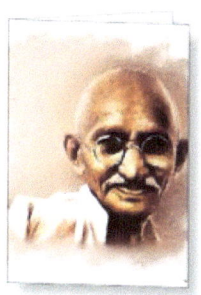

Stretched Canvases		Fine Art Prints		Greeting Cards	
Stretcher Bars: 1.50" x 1.50" or 0.625" x 0.625" Wrap Style: Black, White, or Mirrored Image		Choose From Thousands of Available Frames, Mats, and Fine Art Papers		All Cards are 5" x 7" and Include White Envelopes for Mailing and Gift Giving	
10.25" x 12.00"	$98.86	10.25" x 12.00"	$42.00	Single Card	$4.45 / Card
11.88" x 14.00"	$108.86	11.88" x 14.00"	$55.50	Pack of 10	$2.30 / Card
13.63" x 16.00"	$137.17	13.63" x 16.00"	$74.00	Pack of 25	$1.60 / Card
Prices shown for 1.50" x 1.50" gallery-wrapped prints with black sides.		Prices shown for unframed / unmatted prints on archival matte paper.			

Scan With Smartphone
to Buy Online

Helen Keller
HELEN KELLER (1880-1968)

Helen Keller (1880-1968) was blind, mute and deaf' from a disease which she contracted as a 19-month old baby, yet she accomplished more in her lifetime than many of us blessed with sight, speech and hearing. She was an American author, political activist, lecturer and poet. She was the first deaf-blind person to earn a Bachelor of Arts degree. She also campaigned for women's labor rights during her lifetime. Her accomplishments are remarkable for someone who was blind, mute and deaf. Her life inspires me to be the best I can in spite of obstacles. I think she inspires us all. Here is my portrait of her in pencil.

"Museums and art stores are also sources of pleasure and inspiration. Doubtless it will seem strange to many that the hand unaided by sight can feel action, sentiment, beauty in the cold marble..."

— Helen Keller (1880-1968), U.S. blind/deaf author, lecturer. The Story of My Life, pt. 1, ch. 22 (1903)

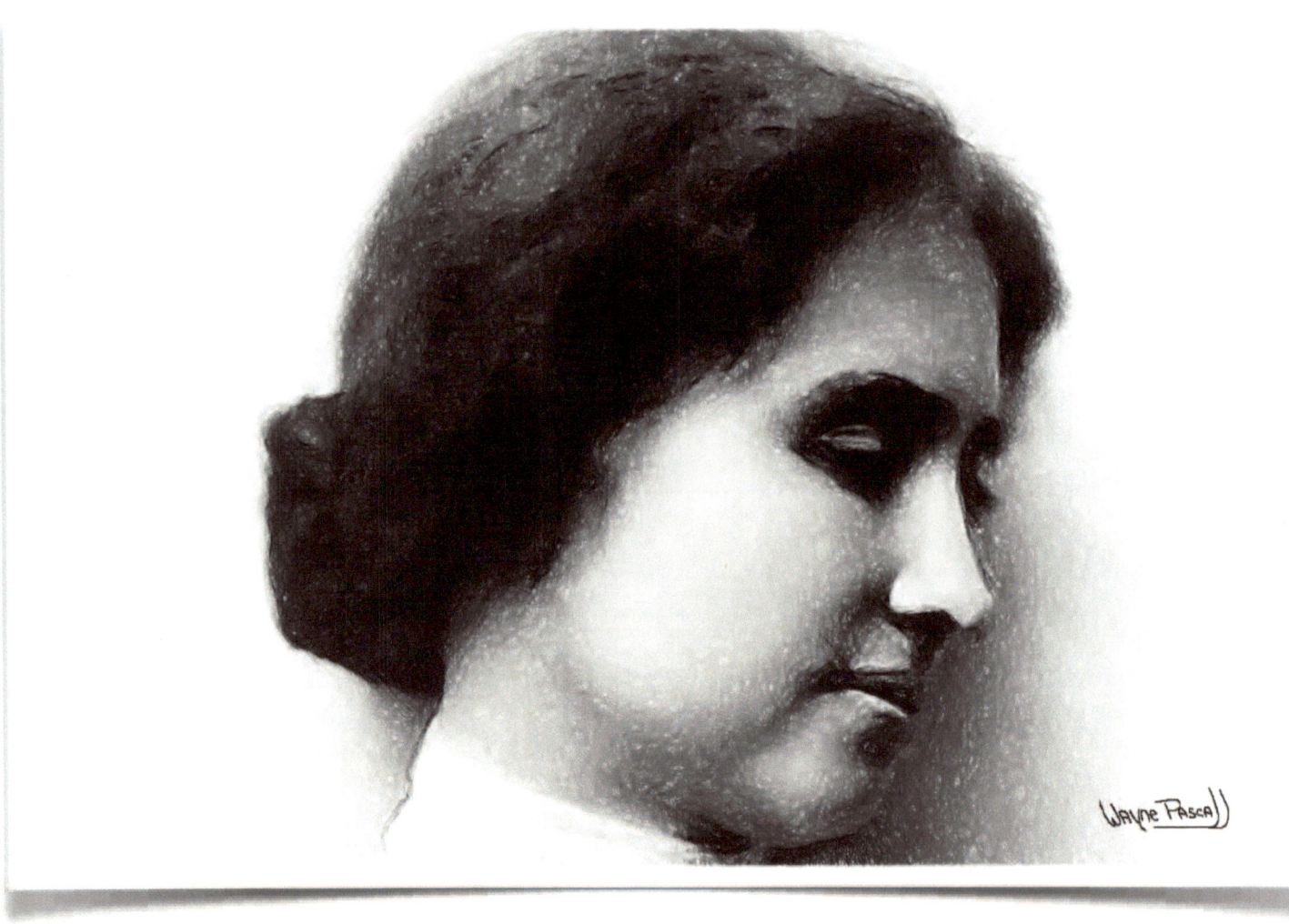

Helen Keller

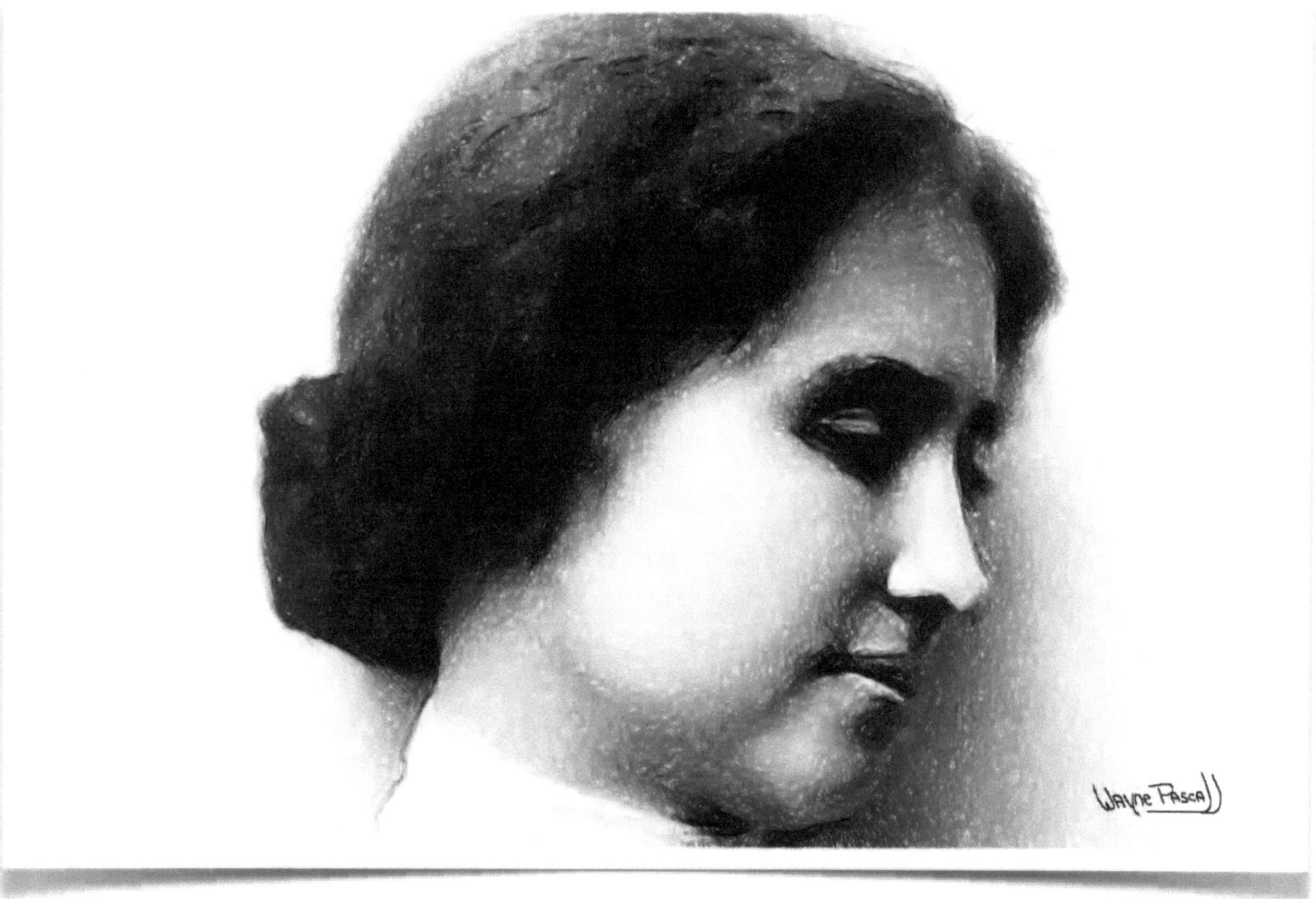

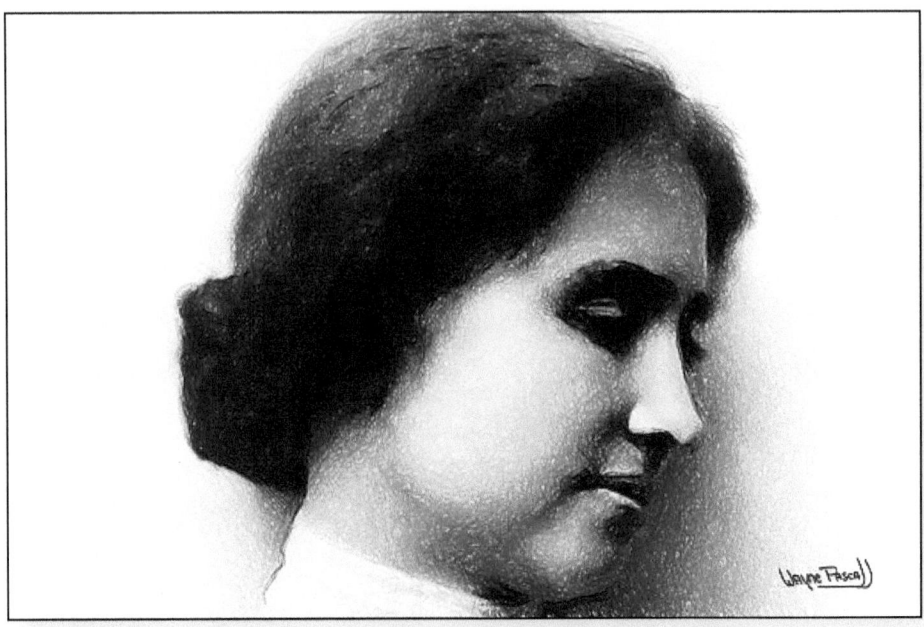

Helen Keller

Wayne Pascall

http://wayne-pascall.artistwebsites.com/featured/helen-keller-wayne-pascall.html

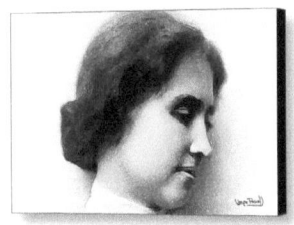 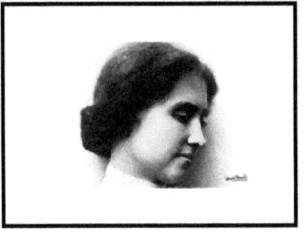 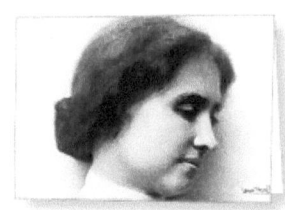

Stretched Canvases

Stretcher Bars: 1.50" x 1.50" or 0.625" x 0.625"
Wrap Style: Black, White, or Mirrored Image

10.00" x 6.38"	$69.96
12.00" x 7.75"	$71.96
14.00" x 9.00"	$90.86
16.00" x 10.25"	$93.86

Prices shown for 1.50" x 1.50" gallery-wrapped
prints with black sides.

Fine Art Prints

Choose From Thousands of Available
Frames, Mats, and Fine Art Papers

8.00" x 5.13"	$22.00
10.00" x 6.38"	$27.00
12.00" x 7.75"	$29.00
14.00" x 9.00"	$34.00
16.00" x 10.25"	$40.50

Prices shown for unframed / unmatted
prints on archival matte paper.

Greeting Cards

All Cards are 5" x 7" and Include
White Envelopes for Mailing and Gift Giving

Single Card	$4.45 / Card
Pack of 10	$2.30 / Card
Pack of 25	$1.75 / Card

Scan With Smartphone
to Buy Online

Florence Nightingale

FLORENCE NIGHTINGALE

"THE LADY WITH THE LAMP" (1820-1910)

The life of this remarkable woman inspires me. Born in 1820 of a wealthy family and also known as "The Lady with The Lamp," Florence Nightingale rejected an affluent lifestyle for a life of servitude in taking care of the sick and wounded soldiers. She is credited as being the mother of the nursing profession and her well-documented nursing techniques are still being implemented in the nursing profession to this day. She was also a celebrated English social reformer and statistician. Florence died in her sleep at the age of 90. The life of this remarkable woman inspires me. Here is my portrait of her in pencil.

Art Meets Science
The life and work of Florence Nightingale is very intriguing. Not only did she voluntarily forgo a life of affluence for one of selfless servitude but she was also brilliant and artistic at the same time. Her diagrams from her nursing practice reveals a statistical brilliant mind that displayed her research in artistic diagrams. The Polar-Area diagram was invented by Florence Nightingale. Florence Nightingale was the first person to use diagrams to persuade people of the need for change. This part of her work where art met science, revealed the catastrophe when most of the British soldiers died from preventable causes - disease.

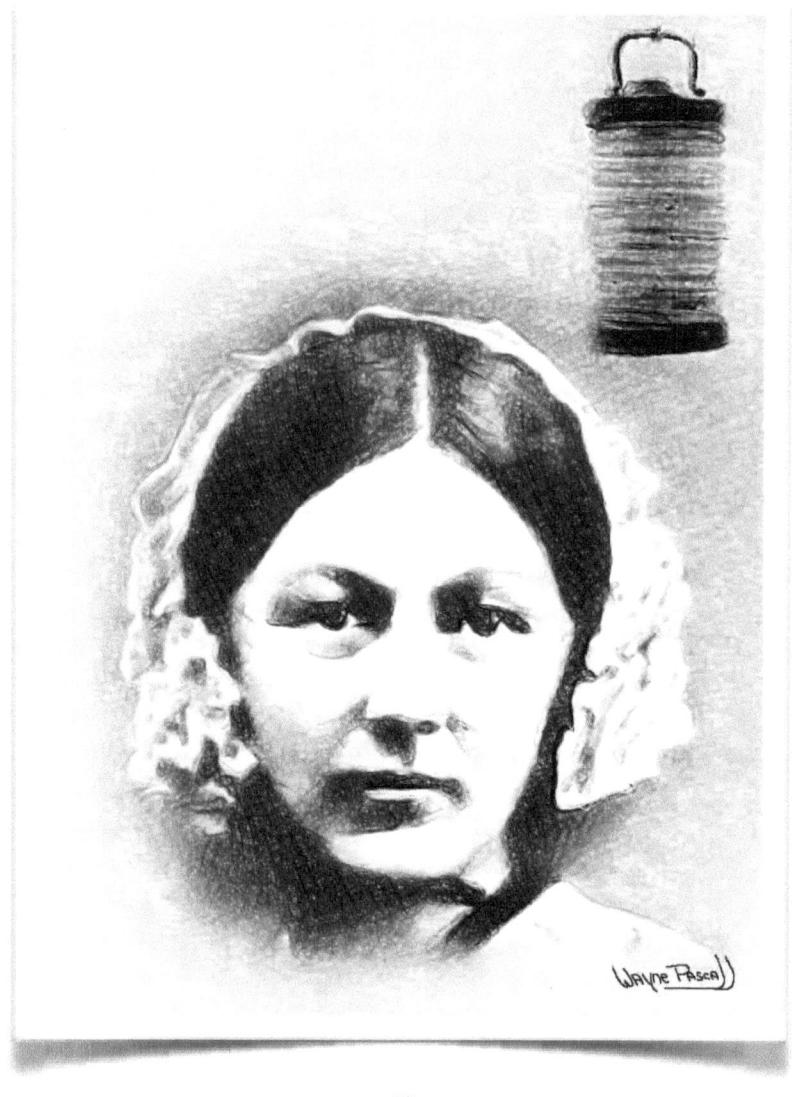

19

Florence Nightingale

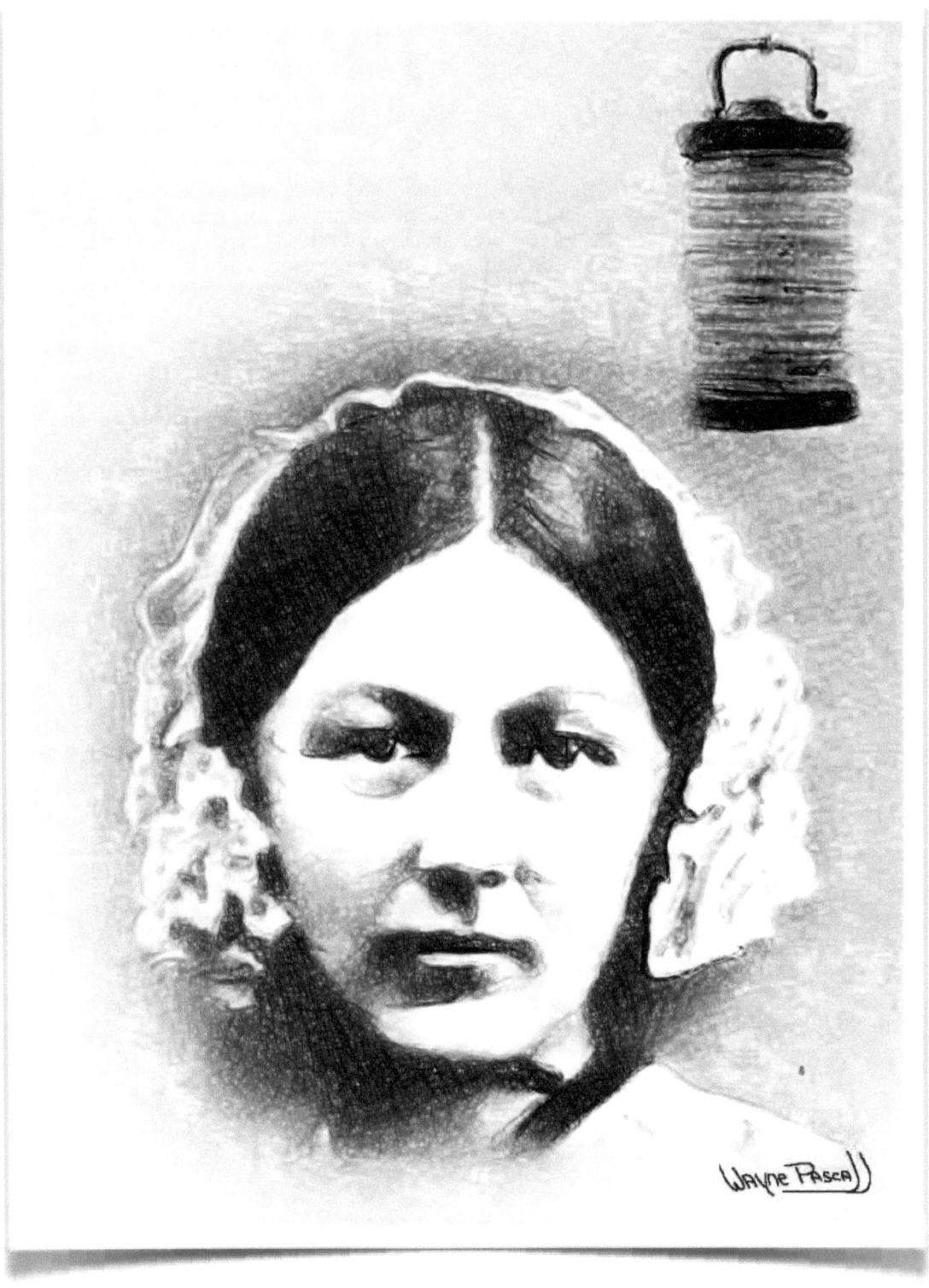

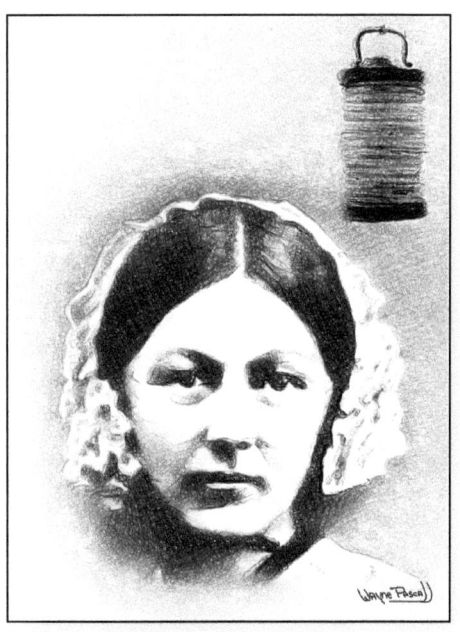

Lady with The Lamp - Florence
Wayne Pascall

http://wayne-pascall.artistwebsites.com/featured/lady-with-the-lamp-florence-wayne-pascall.html

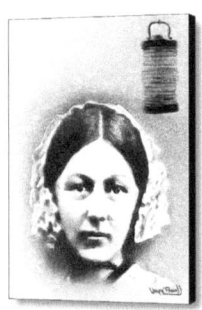 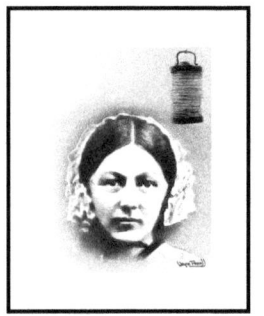 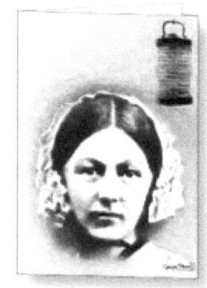

Stretched Canvases		Fine Art Prints		Greeting Cards	
Stretcher Bars: 1.50" x 1.50" or 0.625" x 0.625" Wrap Style: Black, White, or Mirrored Image		Choose From Thousands of Available Frames, Mats, and Fine Art Papers		All Cards are 5" x 7" and Include White Envelopes for Mailing and Gift Giving	
6.00" x 8.00"	$47.04	6.00" x 8.00"	$22.00	Single Card	$4.45 / Card
7.50" x 10.00"	$69.96	7.50" x 10.00"	$27.00	Pack of 10	$2.30 / Card
9.00" x 12.00"	$71.96	9.00" x 12.00"	$29.00	Pack of 25	$1.75 / Card
10.50" x 14.00"	$90.86	10.50" x 14.00"	$37.50		
12.00" x 16.00"	$107.17	12.00" x 16.00"	$40.50		

Prices shown for 1.50" x 1.50" gallery-wrapped prints with black sides.

Prices shown for unframed / unmatted prints on archival matte paper.

Scan With Smartphone
to Buy Online

Nelson Mandela
NELSON MANDELA (1918-2013)

Nelson Mandela, also called "Madiba", led the struggle to replace South Africa's apartheid system with a multi-racial democracy He was persecuted for his early efforts and dedication to this cause by being imprisoned for 27 years.. After a his release from prison, Nelson Mandela resumed his activities with the ANC party. Negotiations between him and De Clerk and after gaining leadership of the party, he and De Clerk brought sweeping changes including the integration of equal voting rights and multiracial elections,. This ultimately led to Mandela's victory in 1994 as the new president of South Africa.

"It always seem impossible until it's done" — Nelson Mandela

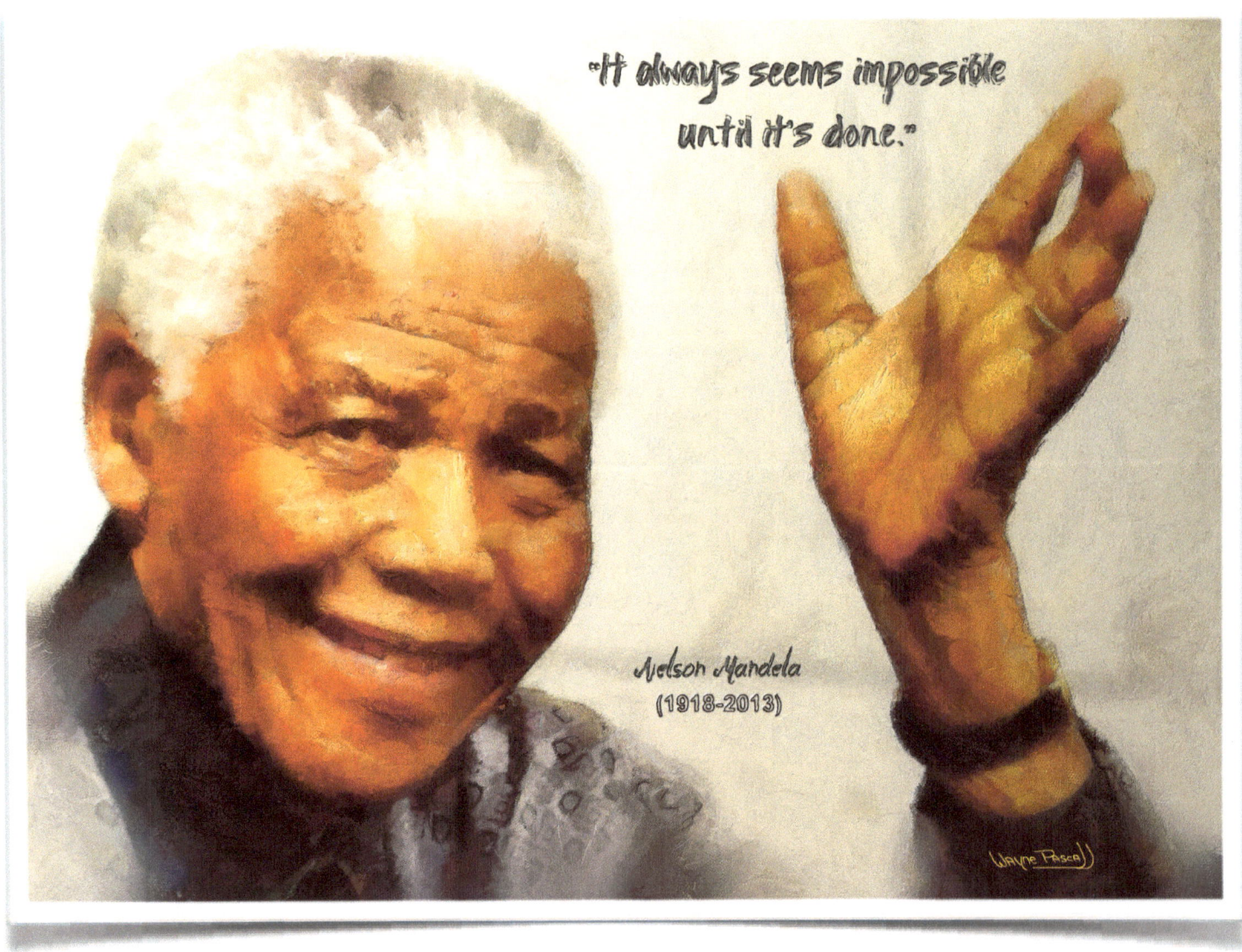

Nelson Mandela

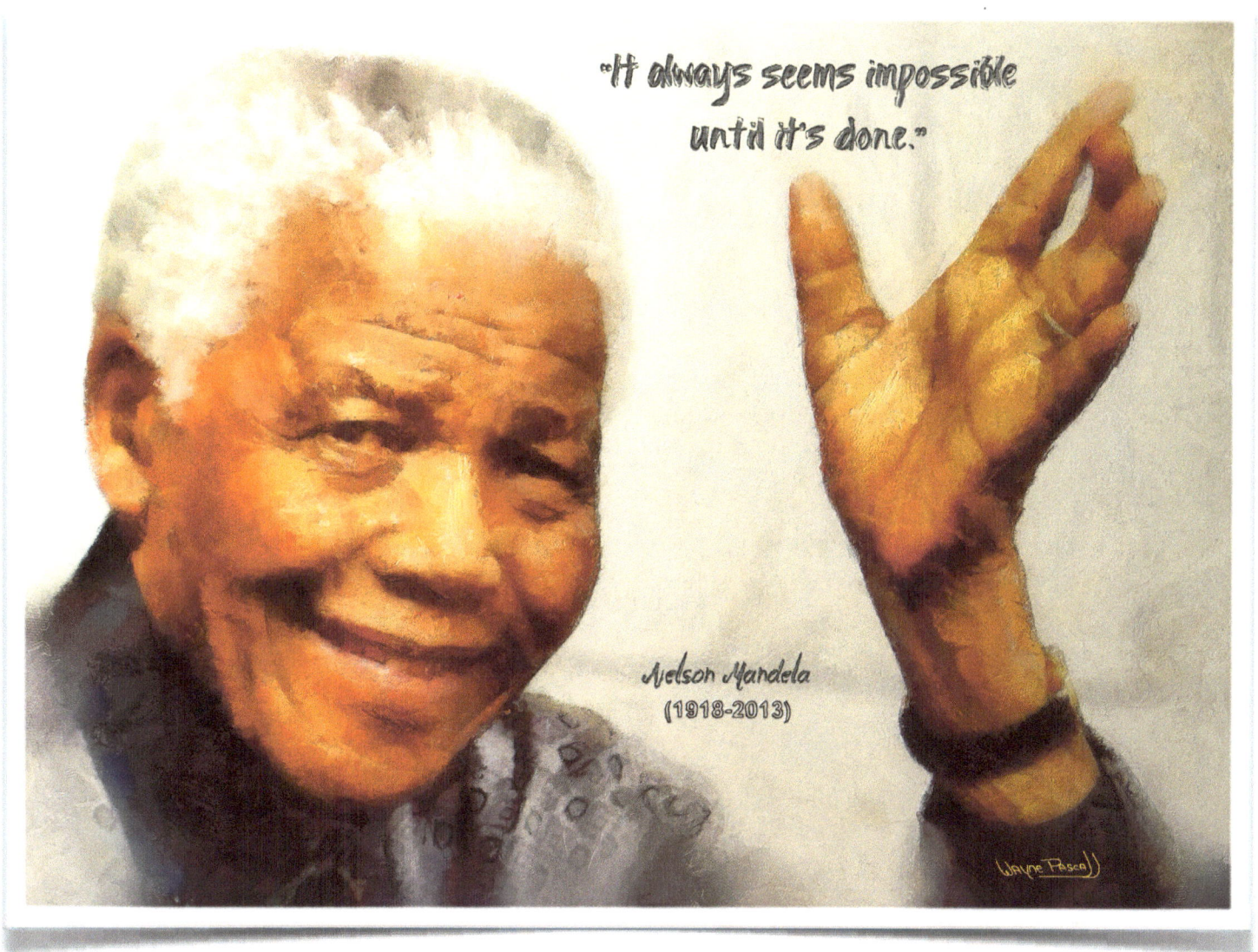

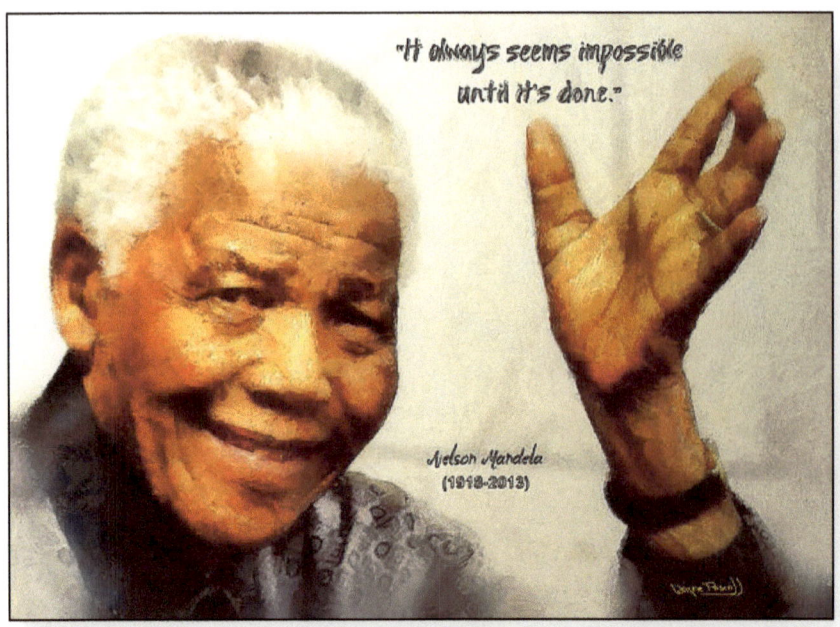

Mandela Farewell
Wayne Pascall

http://wayne-pascall.artistwebsites.com/featured/mandela-farewell-wayne-pascall.html

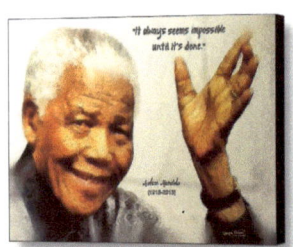
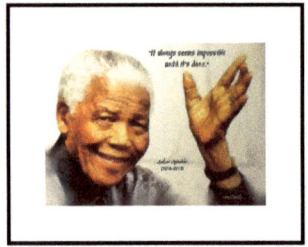
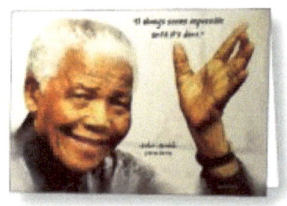

Stretched Canvases		Fine Art Prints		Greeting Cards	
Stretcher Bars: 1.50" x 1.50" or 0.625" x 0.625" Wrap Style: Black, White, or Mirrored Image		Choose From Thousands of Available Frames, Mats, and Fine Art Papers		All Cards are 5" x 7" and Include White Envelopes for Mailing and Gift Giving	
10.00" x 7.13"	$74.96	8.00" x 5.75"	$27.00	Single Card	$4.45 / Card
12.00" x 8.63"	$84.96	10.00" x 7.13"	$32.00	Pack of 10	$2.30 / Card
14.00" x 10.00"	$108.86	12.00" x 8.63"	$42.00	Pack of 25	$1.60 / Card
16.00" x 11.50"	$137.17	14.00" x 10.00"	$52.00		
20.00" x 14.25"	$217.41	16.00" x 11.50"	$70.50		
24.00" x 17.13"	$296.26	20.00" x 14.25"	$129.00		
30.00" x 21.50"	$395.94	24.00" x 17.13"	$191.00		
36.00" x 25.75"	$492.65	30.00" x 21.50"	$256.50		
40.00" x 28.63"	$577.42	36.00" x 25.75"	$330.05		
48.00" x 34.38"	$706.87	40.00" x 28.63"	$396.60		
		48.00" x 34.38"	$478.55		

Prices shown for 1.50" x 1.50" gallery-wrapped prints with black sides.

Prices shown for unframed / unmatted prints on archival matte paper.

Scan With Smartphone to Buy Online

JESUS THE CHRIST (A.D. – ANNO DOMINI)

Throughout the life of Jesus The Christ, **Augustus Caesar** and **Tiberius Caesar** were the emperors of the Roman empire, while **Herod Archaleus, Antipas** ruled the Jews as an official of Rome. During his relatively short life of 33 years, Jesus The Christ announced to the world that he was The Son of the most high God, sent to redeem the world from sin. His teachings and details of his life are written in the Gospels of The Holy Bible and believed by Christians all over the world. During his life, Jesus Christ not only performed acts of kindness to sick and disabled human beings in the form of miracles, but he also called and discipled people dedicated to following him and his ways. Of his many disciples, he chose 12 whom he called Apostles. He charged them with the great commission of taking his "**gospel**" or "**good news**" about salvation from sin, to the whole world. The community of saved believers was and is called the "**church**" or "**called out**". Scribes, Pharisees and Jewish high priests in his time accused him of heresy and using a traitor named Judas, had him tried before Pontius Pilate and executed by crucifixion – An act which The Holy Bible claims was part of Divine destiny.

The life of Jesus The Christ has impacted the world in so many positive ways, implementing a system of ethics that complemented the Judaistic doctrines found in the Old Testament of the Holy Bible. Our current date, example: 2014, is tagged with the letters A.D. at the end; an abbreviation for "**Anno Domini**" . It means "**In the year of The Lord**." Our current date signifies the amount time elapsed since the birth of Jesus The Christ. Time is either rendered as B.C. (Before Christ) or A.D. (After Christ) No other individual has ever had that kind of impact on the world.

"I am the way, and the truth and the life. No one comes to the Father except through me" — Jesus Christ

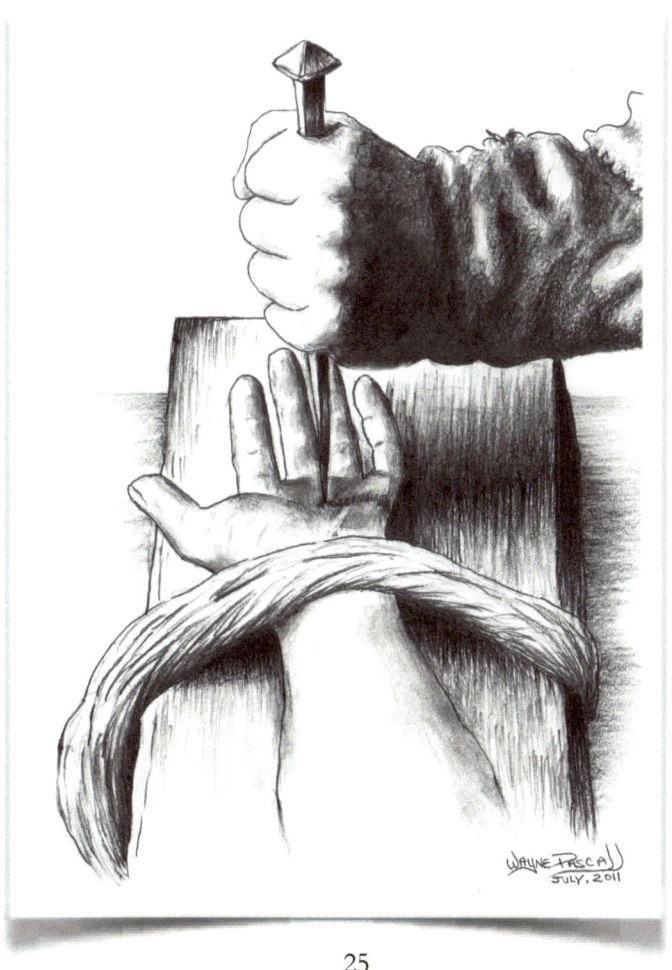

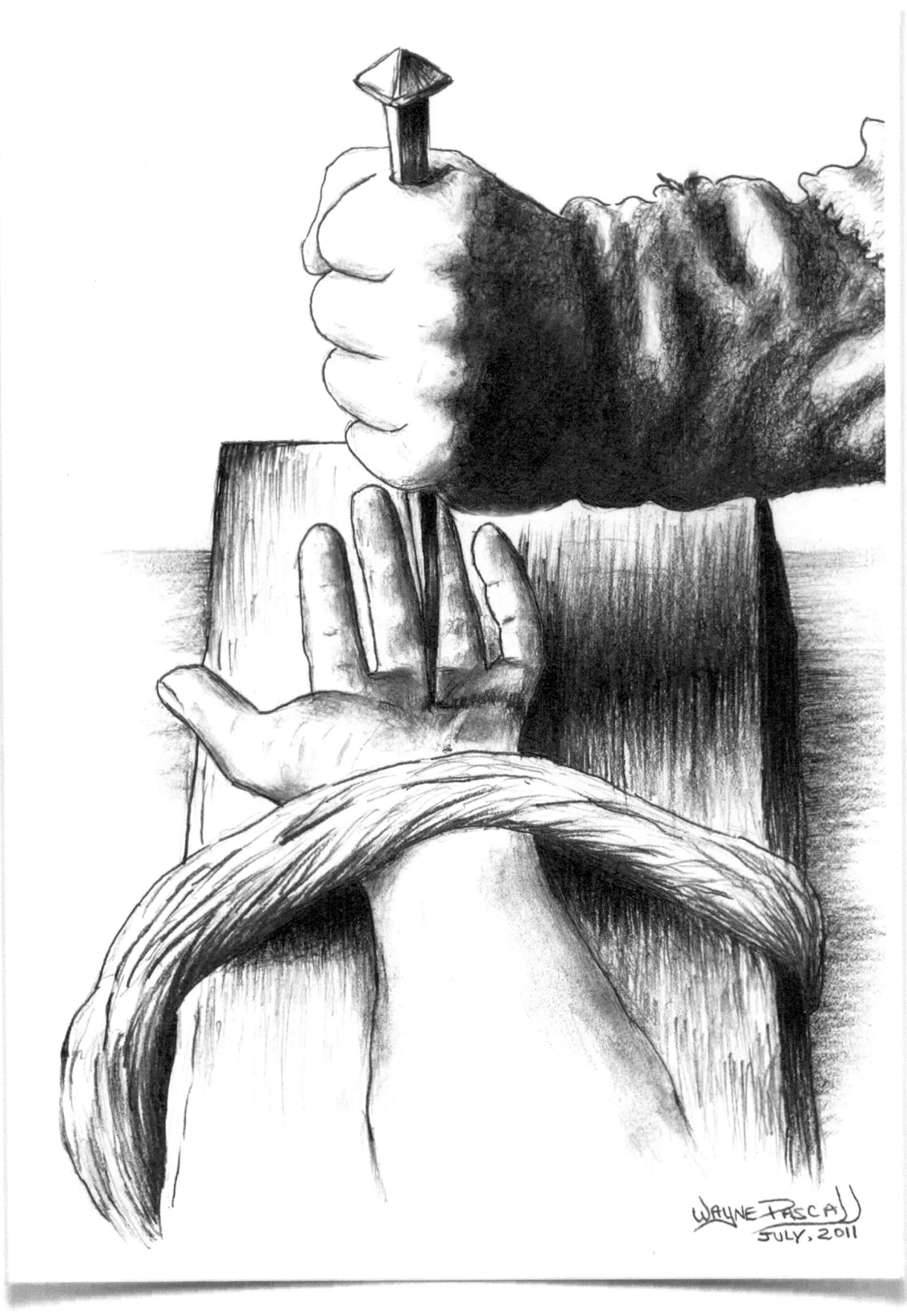

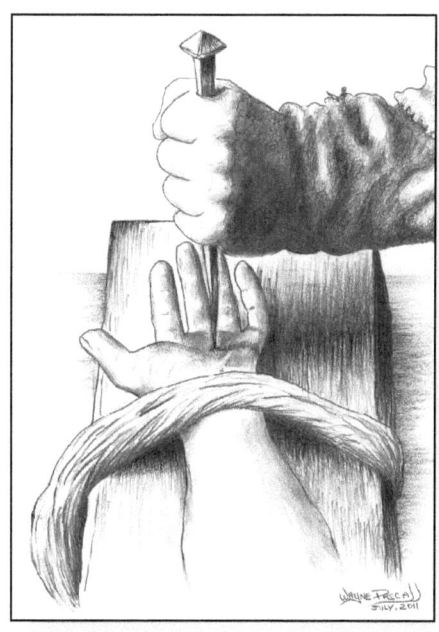

Pierced

Wayne Pascall

http://wayne-pascall.artistwebsites.com/featured/pierced-wayne-pascall.html

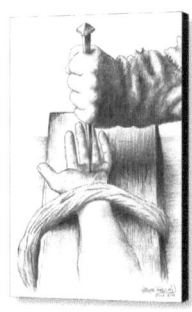

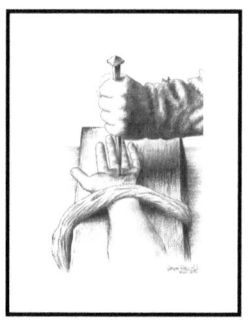

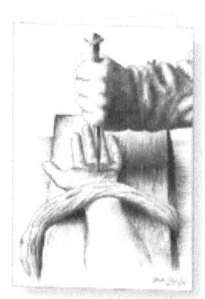

Stretched Canvases

Stretcher Bars: 1.50" x 1.50" or 0.625" x 0.625"
Wrap Style: Black, White, or Mirrored Image

7.25" x 10.00"	$65.96
8.63" x 12.00"	$66.96
10.13" x 14.00"	$82.86
11.50" x 16.00"	$97.17
14.38" x 20.00"	$123.41
17.25" x 24.00"	$148.26
21.63" x 30.00"	$193.94
25.88" x 36.00"	$237.65
28.88" x 40.00"	$282.08

Prices shown for 1.50" x 1.50" gallery-wrapped
prints with black sides.

Fine Art Prints

Choose From Thousands of Available
Frames, Mats, and Fine Art Papers

5.75" x 8.00"	$22.00
7.25" x 10.00"	$23.00
8.63" x 12.00"	$24.00
10.13" x 14.00"	$26.00
11.50" x 16.00"	$30.50
14.38" x 20.00"	$35.00
17.25" x 24.00"	$43.00
21.63" x 30.00"	$58.00
25.88" x 36.00"	$75.05
28.88" x 40.00"	$95.45

Prices shown for unframed / unmatted
prints on archival matte paper.

Greeting Cards

All Cards are 5" x 7" and Include
White Envelopes for Mailing and Gift Giving

Single Card	$4.95 / Card

Scan With Smartphone
to Buy Online

All prints and greeting cards are produced by Artist Websites (Artist Websites) and come with a 30-day money-back guarantee.
Orders may be placed online via credit card or PayPal. All orders ship within three business days from the AW production facility in North Carolina.

Edward Deming

EDWARD DEMING (1900-1993)

Dr. Edward Deming was known as the father of Total Quality Management (TQM). He was a statistician and a student under the instruction of Walter Shewart. It is said that Deming in his early years as a professor at NYU would not grade his students but would just give them Pass or Fail. His premise was that he did know what they would become in 10 years, which is what should be really measured. Walter Edward Deming believed that effective leadership, at all levels, could only truly be executed when that management understands the job needed to be done at the front line. He believed that quality should be driven from the customer to the support of management at the top. Employees were called associates and empowered to satisfy the customer in an upside down pyramid model.

These ideas were revolutionary in his time and Deming's quality principles at first were not warmly accepted in the United States. In 1950 Japanese business leaders invited Deming to Japan to teach executives and engineers about his new quality methods. Japanese companies quickly adopted his principles, with the result being a commitment to quality control that helped Japanese firms dominate some product markets in many parts of the world. The Deming Prize, established 1951, was awarded annually to Japanese corporations that win a rigorous quality-control competition,. It was not until the 1980s that Deming's ideas were adopted by American corporations seeking to compete with the Japanese success.

"It is not enough to do your best; you must know what to do, and then do your best." — Edward Deming

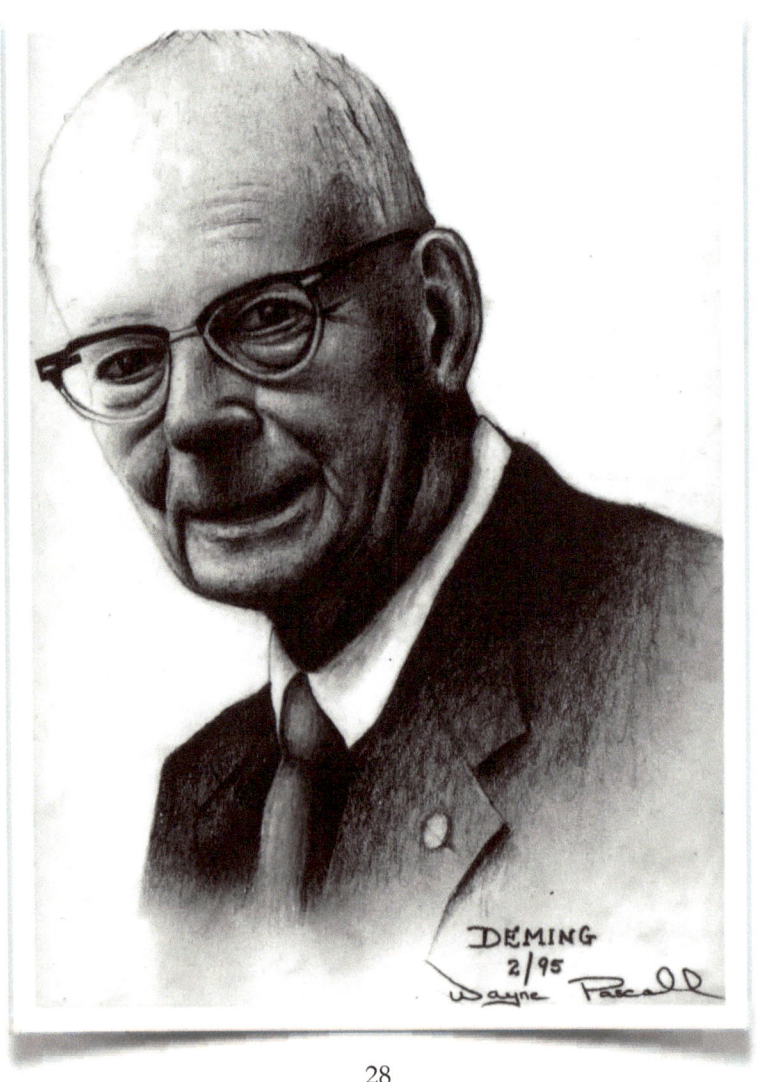

Edward Deming

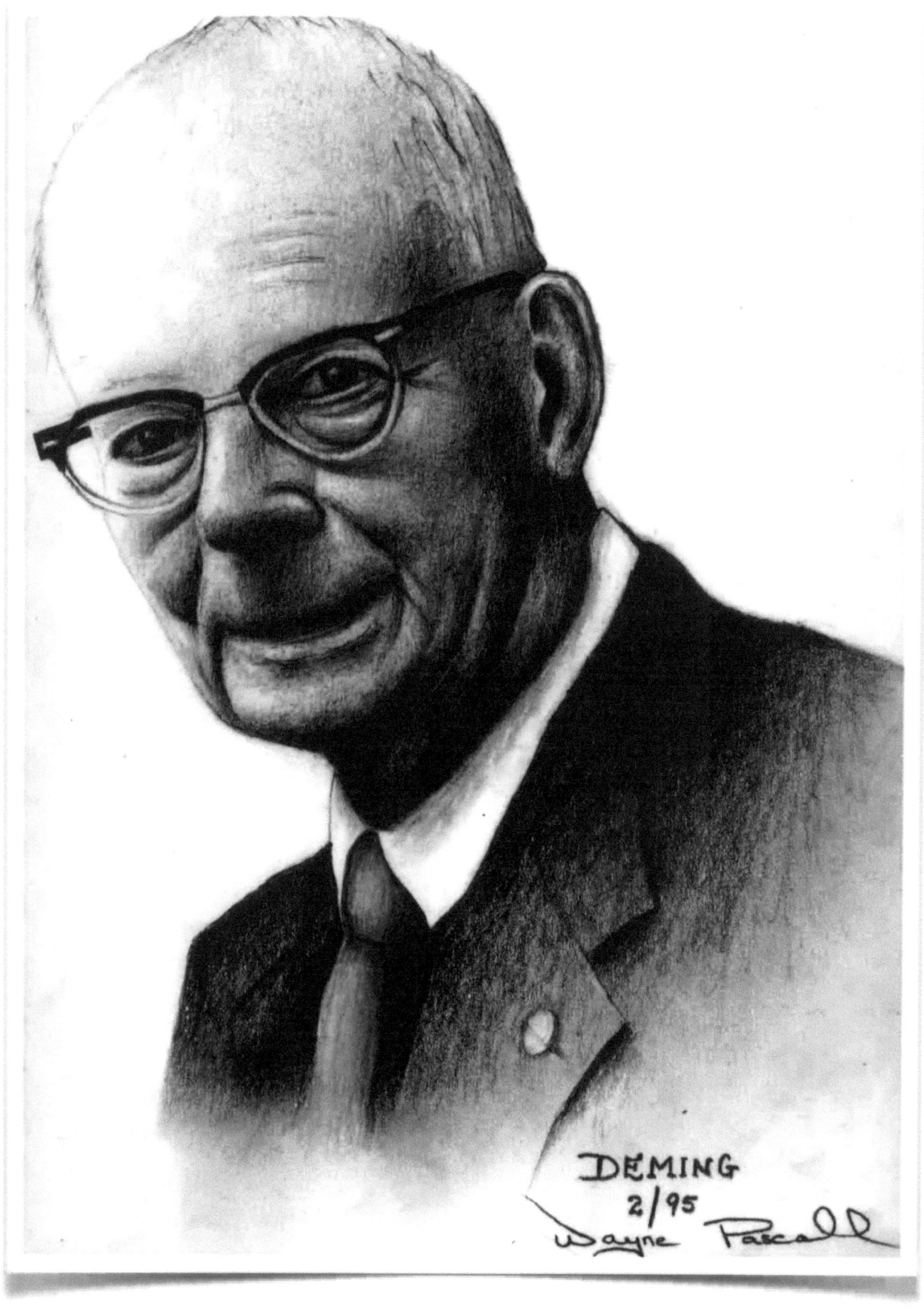

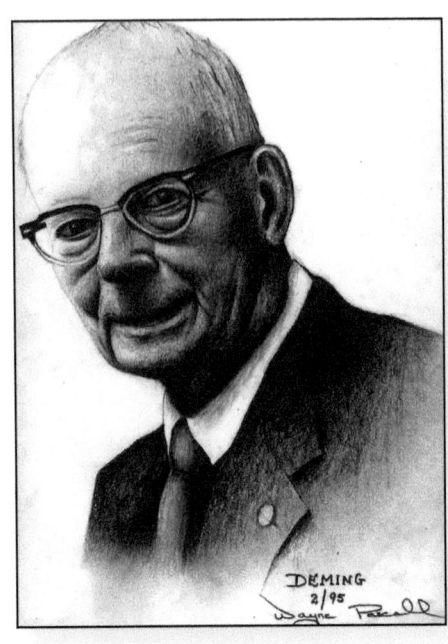

Deming

Wayne Pascall

http://wayne-pascall.artistwebsites.com/featured/deming-wayne-pascall.html

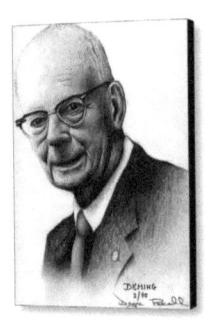

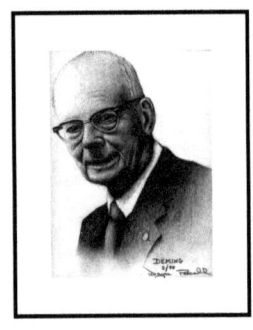

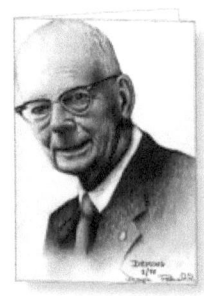

Stretched Canvases

Stretcher Bars: 1.50" x 1.50" or 0.625" x 0.625"
Wrap Style: Black, White, or Mirrored Image

7.38" x 10.00"	$74.96
8.75" x 12.00"	$84.96
10.25" x 14.00"	$108.86
11.75" x 16.00"	$137.17
14.63" x 20.00"	$217.41
17.63" x 24.00"	$296.26
22.00" x 30.00"	$395.94
26.38" x 36.00"	$492.65
29.38" x 40.00"	$587.08
35.25" x 48.00"	$715.75

Prices shown for 1.50" x 1.50" gallery-wrapped
prints with black sides.

Fine Art Prints

Choose From Thousands of Available
Frames, Mats, and Fine Art Papers

5.88" x 8.00"	$27.00
7.38" x 10.00"	$32.00
8.75" x 12.00"	$42.00
10.25" x 14.00"	$52.00
11.75" x 16.00"	$70.50
14.63" x 20.00"	$132.50
17.63" x 24.00"	$191.00
22.00" x 30.00"	$260.00
26.38" x 36.00"	$333.90
29.38" x 40.00"	$400.45

Visit website for larger sizes.
Prices shown for unframed / unmatted
prints on archival matte paper.

Greeting Cards

All Cards are 5" x 7" and Include
White Envelopes for Mailing and Gift Giving

Single Card	$4.45 / Card
Pack of 10	$2.30 / Card
Pack of 25	$1.60 / Card

Scan With Smartphone
to Buy Online

MARTIN LUTHER KING JR. (1929-1968)

Martin Luther King Jr. was a Baptist minister, born on January 15, 1929 in Atlanta, Georgia. King also became a social activist playing an integral role in the American civil rights movement from the mid-1950s to his assassination in 1968. Dr. King got some of his inspiration from his predecessor, Mahatma Gandhi, who used nonviolent and peaceful resistance to galvanize change. King sought equality for African Americans, all the economically disadvantaged and victims of injustice using peaceful protests. His vision was that America and all the world could become a colorblind society where race would not impede a person's civil rights. His life's work resulted in legislation such as the Civil Rights Act of 1964 and the Voting Rights Act of 1965. In 1964, King was awarded the prestige Nobel Peace Prize. His legacy and life is remembered each year on Martin Luther King Jr. Day, declared a U.S. federal holiday since 1986. He is considered one of the greatest orators of modern times and his speeches still inspire many to this day.

"Darkness cannot drive out darkness; only light can do that. Hate cannot drive out hate; only love can do that."
— Dr. Martin Luther King Jr.

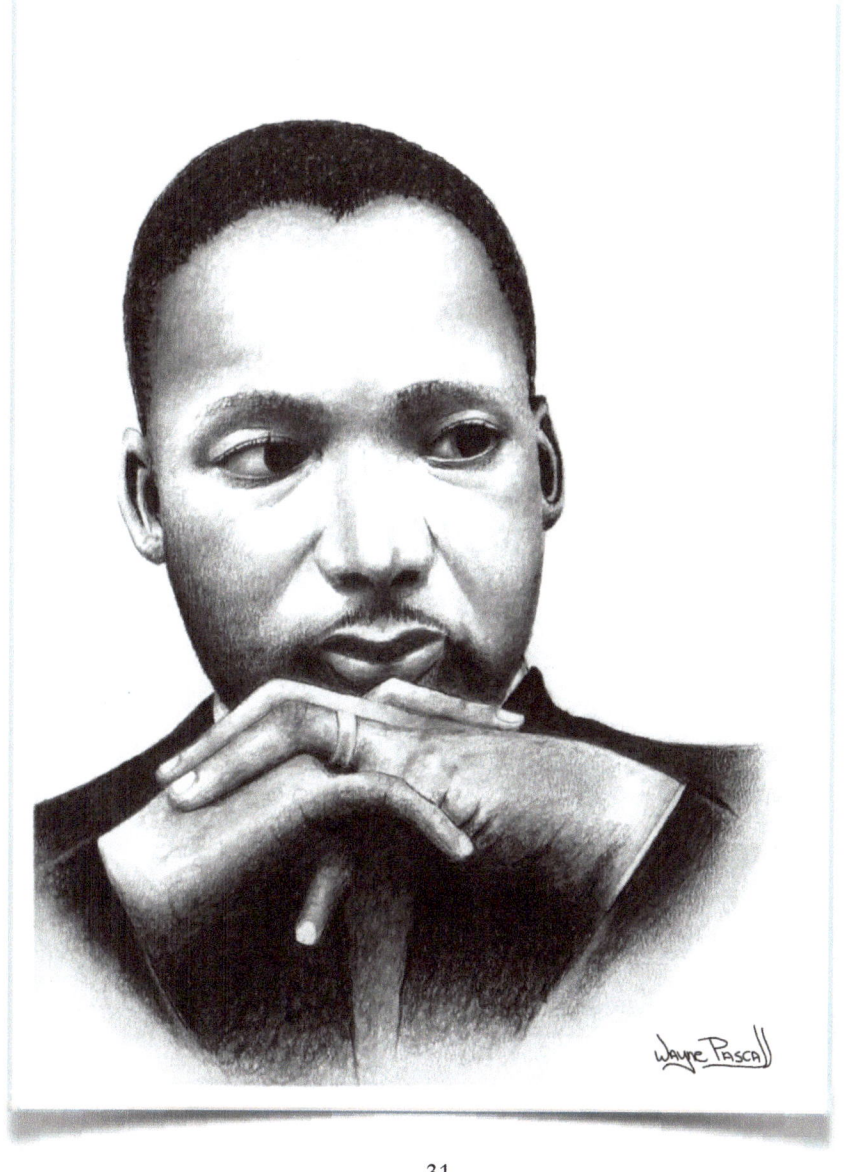

Martin Luther King Jr.

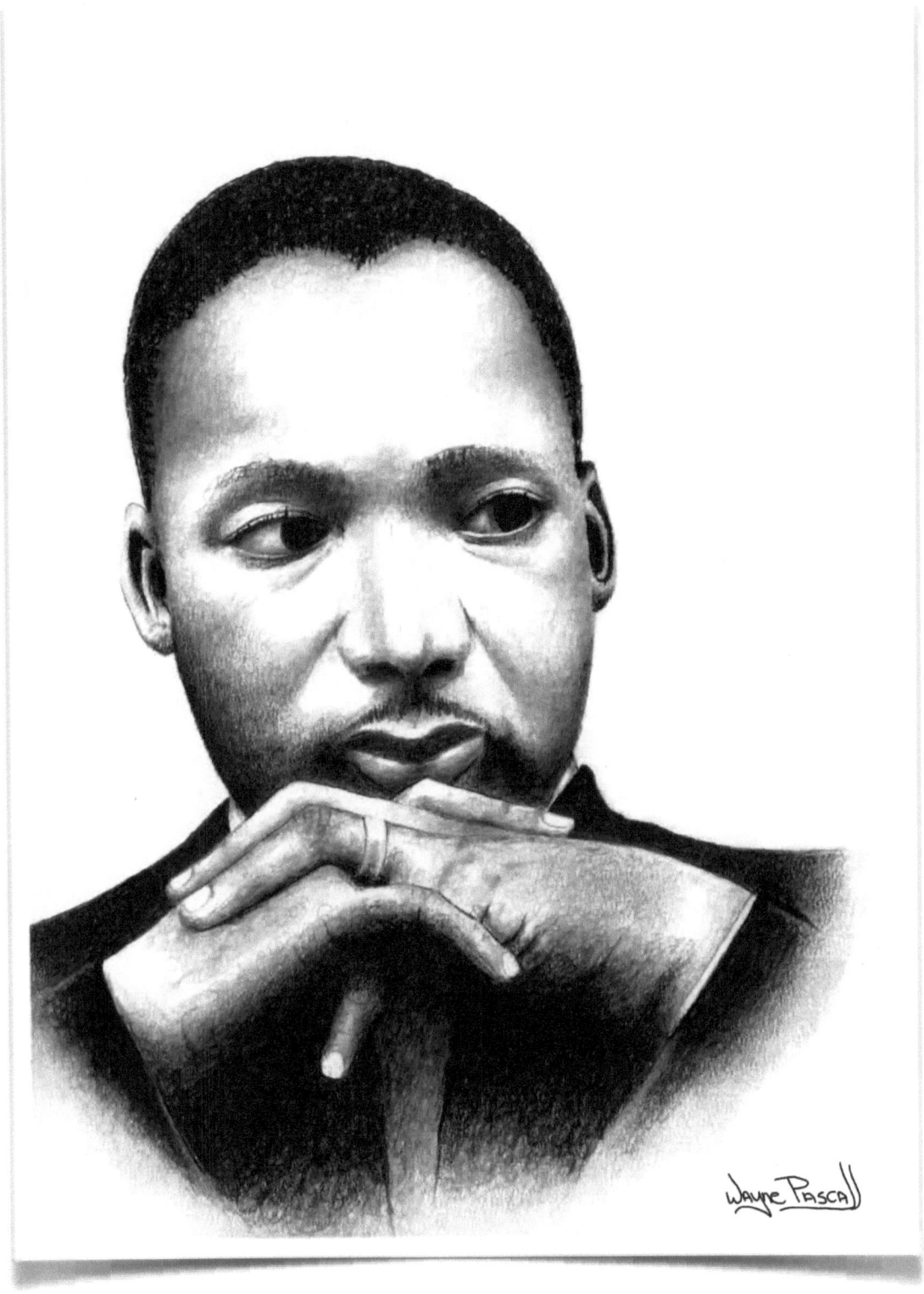

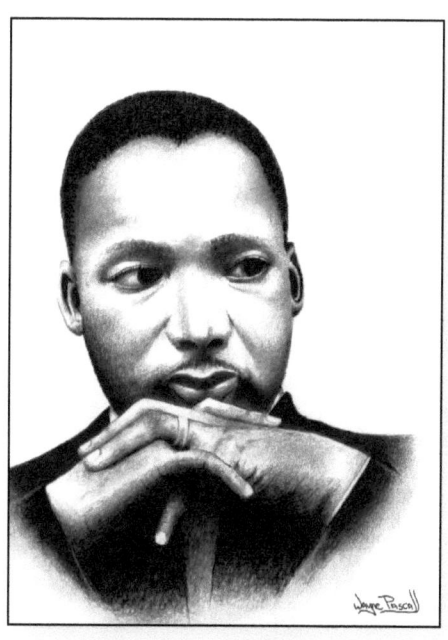

Martin
Wayne Pascall

http://wayne-pascall.artistwebsites.com/featured/martin-wayne-pascall.html

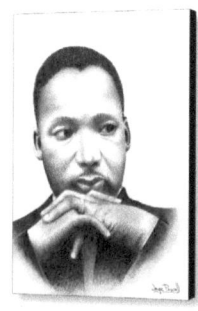
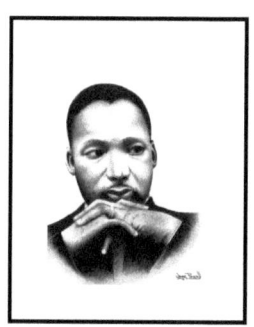
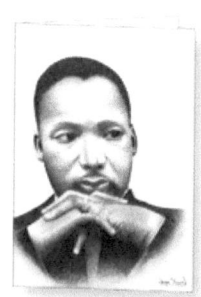

Stretched Canvases

Stretcher Bars: 1.50" x 1.50" or 0.625" x 0.625"
Wrap Style: Black, White, or Mirrored Image

7.38" x 10.00"	$65.96
8.75" x 12.00"	$68.96
11.75" x 16.00"	$97.67
14.63" x 20.00"	$124.41
17.63" x 24.00"	$149.76
22.00" x 30.00"	$195.94
26.38" x 36.00"	$239.15
29.38" x 40.00"	$280.08
35.25" x 48.00"	$355.75

Prices shown for 1.50" x 1.50" gallery-wrapped
prints with black sides.

Fine Art Prints

Choose From Thousands of Available
Frames, Mats, and Fine Art Papers

5.88" x 8.00"	$22.00
7.38" x 10.00"	$23.00
8.75" x 12.00"	$26.00
11.75" x 16.00"	$31.00
14.63" x 20.00"	$39.50
17.63" x 24.00"	$44.50
22.00" x 30.00"	$60.00
26.38" x 36.00"	$80.40
29.38" x 40.00"	$93.45
35.25" x 48.00"	$122.40

Prices shown for unframed / unmatted
prints on archival matte paper.

Greeting Cards

All Cards are 5" x 7" and Include
White Envelopes for Mailing and Gift Giving

Single Card	$4.95 / Card
Pack of 10	$2.70 / Card
Pack of 25	$2.00 / Card

Scan With Smartphone
to Buy Online

CHIEF SITTING BULL (1831-1890)

Chief Sitting Bull (1831-1890) whose Indian name was Tatanka Lyotake, was the Indigenous American chief under which the Sioux tribes unified in their battle for survival on the North American Great Plains. Following the revelation of gold in the Black Hills of South Dakota in 1874, the Sioux came into escalated conflicts with the United States authorities. The Great Sioux wars of the 1870s would certainly culminate in the 1876 battle of the Little Bighorn, through which Sitting Bull, Crazy Horse and a group of tribes would defeat government soldiers led by George Armstrong Custer. Sitting bull escaped to Canada but after several years there, he and his people desperate from starvation, eventually surrendered to U.S. authorities. He was finally required to choose a reservation. In 1890, Sitting Bull was shot to death while being detained by U.S. and Indian representatives, afraid that he would assist the expanding Ghost Dance movement aimed at reviving the Sioux way of life. Sitting Bull will always be remembered for his amazing courage and his stubborn determination to stand up to Western domestication of his people.

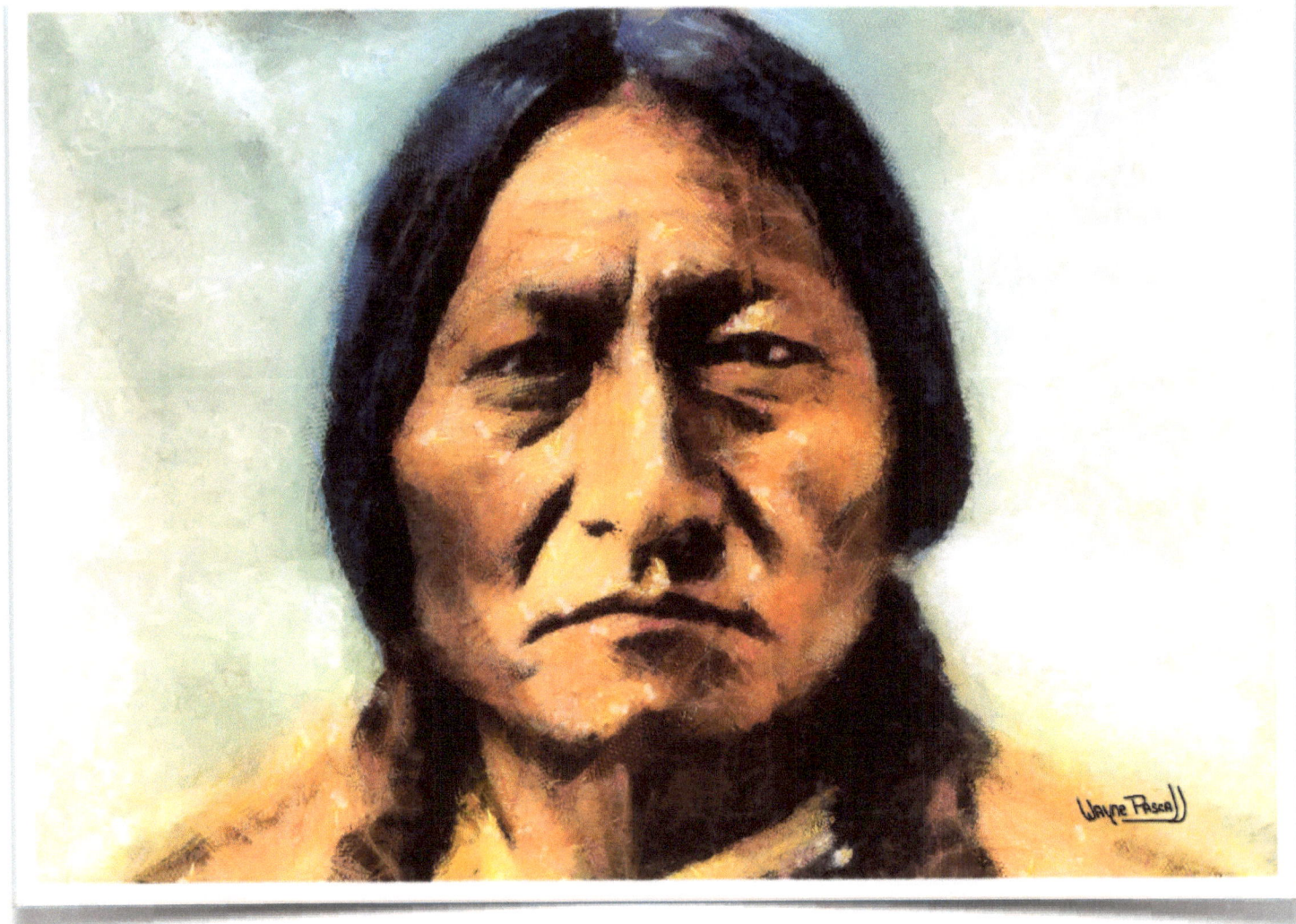

Chief Sitting Bull

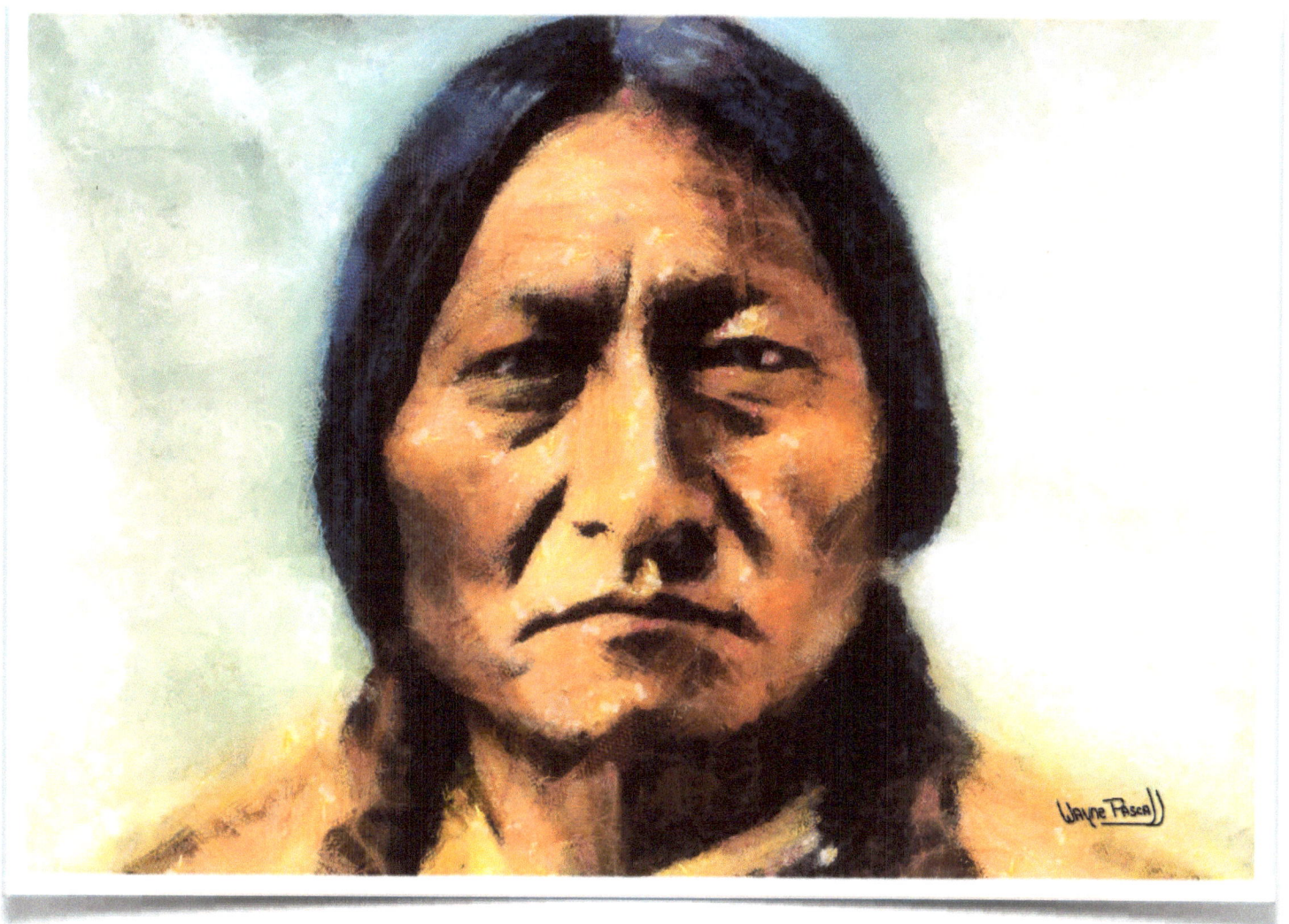

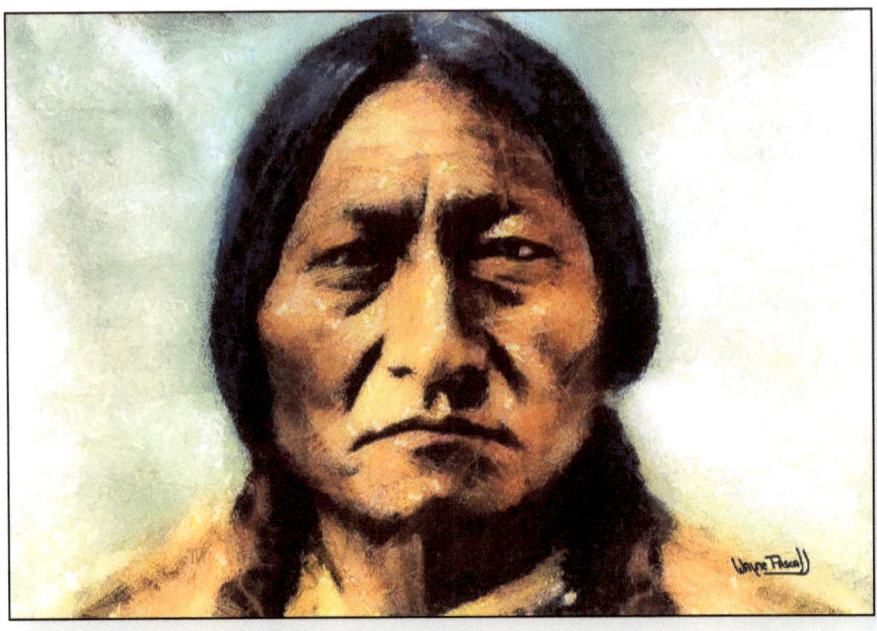

Chief Sitting Bull
Wayne Pascall

http://wayne-pascall.artistwebsites.com/featured/chief-sitting-bull-wayne-pascall.html

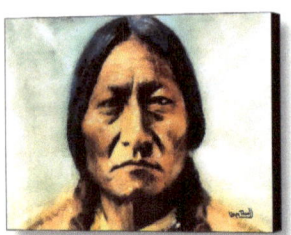

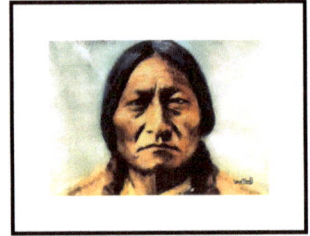

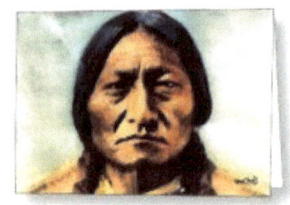

Stretched Canvases

Stretcher Bars: 1.50" x 1.50" or 0.625" x 0.625"
Wrap Style: Black, White, or Mirrored Image

10.00" x 6.75"	$74.96
12.00" x 8.13"	$79.96
14.00" x 9.50"	$93.86
16.00" x 10.88"	$112.17
20.00" x 13.63"	$124.98
24.00" x 16.38"	$154.47

Prices shown for 1.50" x 1.50" gallery-wrapped
prints with black sides.

Fine Art Prints

Choose From Thousands of Available
Frames, Mats, and Fine Art Papers

8.00" x 5.50"	$32.00
10.00" x 6.75"	$32.00
12.00" x 8.13"	$37.00
14.00" x 9.50"	$37.00
16.00" x 10.88"	$45.50
20.00" x 13.63"	$49.00
24.00" x 16.38"	$61.00

Prices shown for unframed / unmatted
prints on archival matte paper.

Greeting Cards

All Cards are 5" x 7" and Include
White Envelopes for Mailing and Gift Giving

Not Available

Scan With Smartphone
to Buy Online

Bob Marley
BOB MARLEY (1945-1981)

Robert Nesta "Bob" Marley (1945 - 1981), was an innovative Jamaican musician who popularized reggae music throughout the world and became one of the most well-known reggae artists ever. Marley was also a cultural revolutionary whose music expressed a fervent longing for political freedom, peace, and racial harmony. The Wailers, comprising of Bob Marley, Bunny Wailer and Peter Tosh disbanded in 1974, Each artist pursued solo careers including Marley. His music as a solo artist culminated in the release of the album Exodus in 1977. This album established his reputation worldwide and he became one of the world's best-selling musicians of all time, with sales of more than 75 million albums and singles. He was a committed Rastafarian who infused his music with a profound sense of spirituality. Many of his songs were social commentaries with spiritual undertones that sought to raise the consciousness of people in general.

"Life is one big road with lots of signs. So when you riding through the ruts, don't complicate your mind. Flee from hate, mischief and jealousy. Don't bury your thoughts, put your vision to reality. Wake Up and Live!"
– Bob Marley

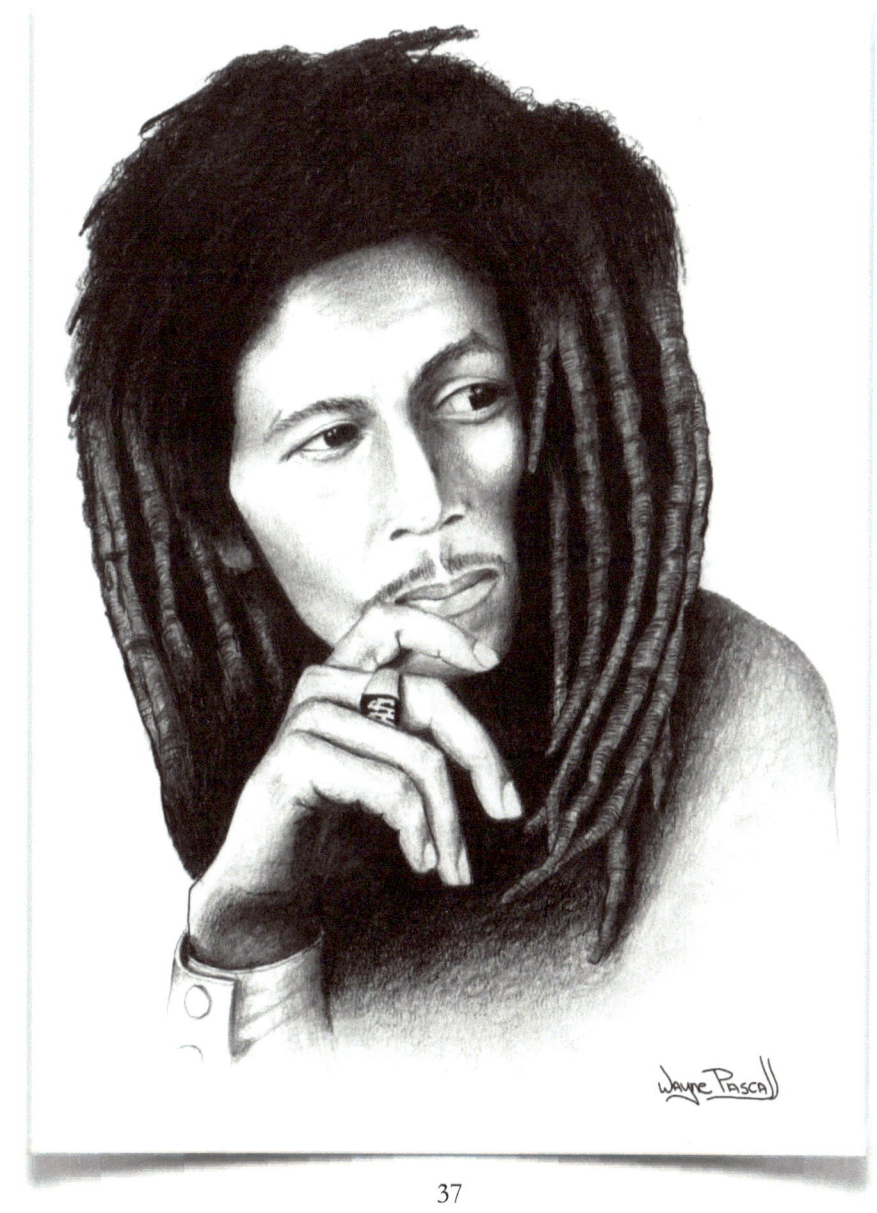

Bob Marley

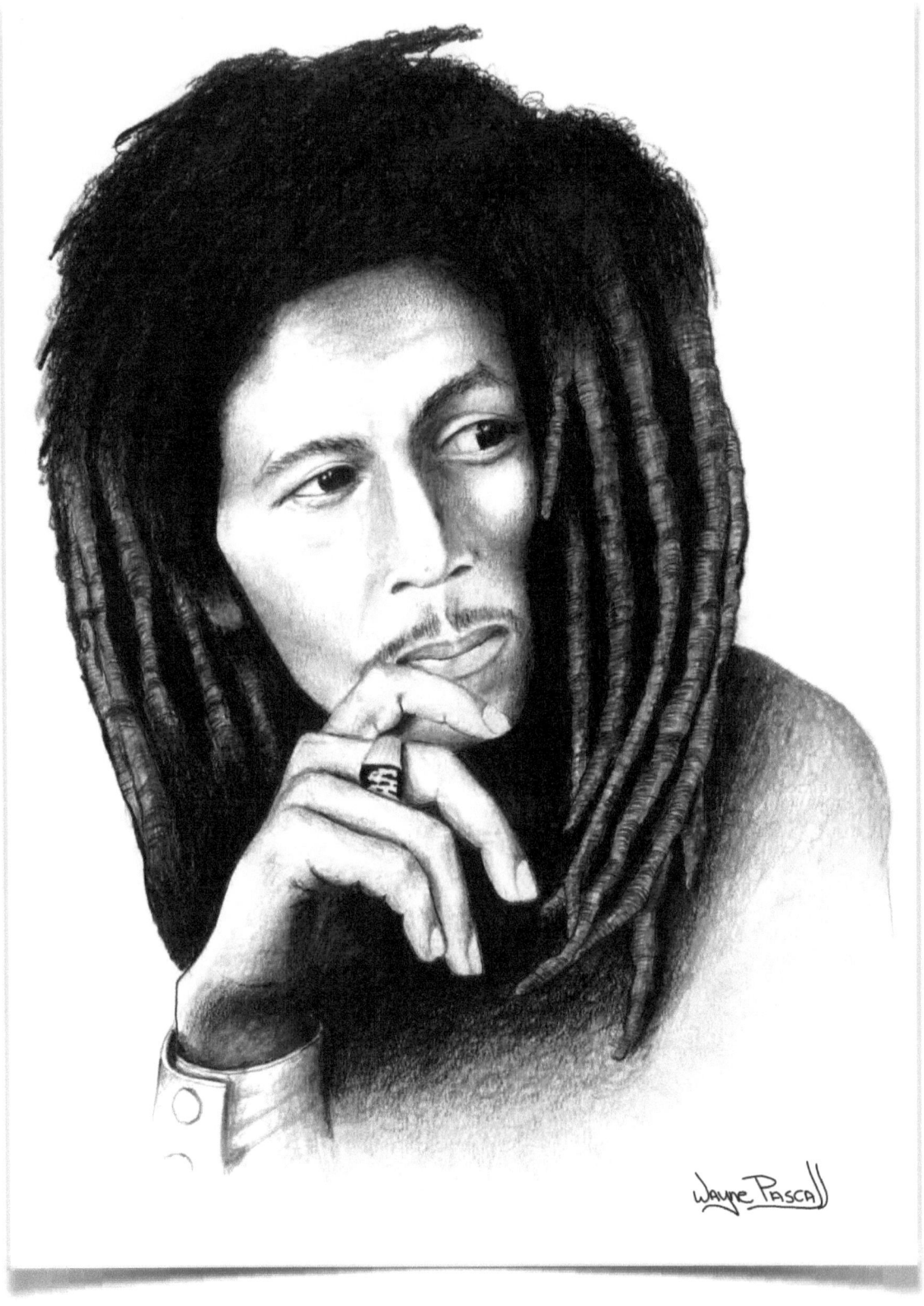

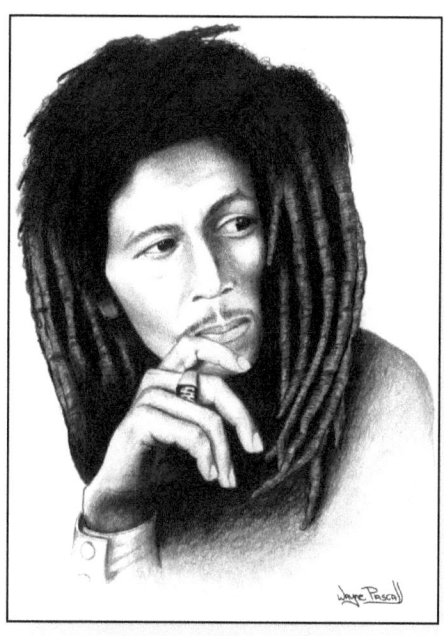

Bob Marley

Wayne Pascall

http://wayne-pascall.artistwebsites.com/featured/bob-marley-wayne-pascall.html

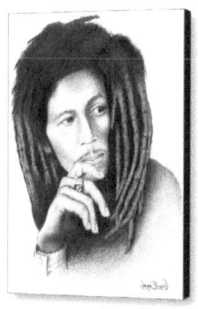

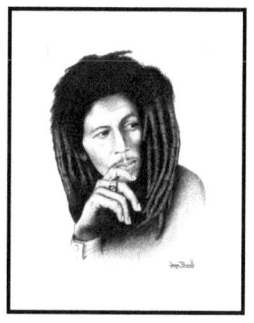

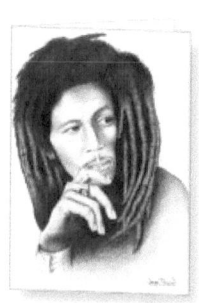

Stretched Canvases

Stretcher Bars: 1.50" x 1.50" or 0.625" x 0.625"
Wrap Style: Black, White, or Mirrored Image

7.38" x 10.00"	$66.46
8.75" x 12.00"	$68.96
11.75" x 16.00"	$97.67
14.63" x 20.00"	$123.91
17.63" x 24.00"	$148.76
22.00" x 30.00"	$194.94
26.38" x 36.00"	$239.15
29.38" x 40.00"	$280.08
35.25" x 48.00"	$355.75

Prices shown for 1.50" x 1.50" gallery-wrapped
prints with black sides.

Fine Art Prints

Choose From Thousands of Available
Frames, Mats, and Fine Art Papers

5.88" x 8.00"	$22.00
7.38" x 10.00"	$23.50
8.75" x 12.00"	$26.00
11.75" x 16.00"	$31.00
14.63" x 20.00"	$39.00
17.63" x 24.00"	$43.50
22.00" x 30.00"	$59.00
26.38" x 36.00"	$80.40
29.38" x 40.00"	$93.45
35.25" x 48.00"	$122.40

Prices shown for unframed / unmatted
prints on archival matte paper.

Greeting Cards

All Cards are 5" x 7" and Include
White Envelopes for Mailing and Gift Giving

Single Card	$4.95 / Card
Pack of 10	$2.70 / Card
Pack of 25	$2.00 / Card

Scan With Smartphone
to Buy Online

Marilyn Monroe
MARILYN MONROE (1926-1962)

Marilyn Monroe is considered a beauty icon and the ultimate sex symbol. As a Hollywood actress, she was graced with physical beauty and charm, but her life was plagued with personal problems. She embodied everything that Hollywood represents: glamor, glitz and sex-appeal. While Marilyn represents everything that is glamorous about Hollywood, she also lived in some of the darkness of Hollywood including scandalous sexual encounters and drug use. Manipulated by high level "mind doctors," who tried to control various aspects of her life, caused Marilyn to spiral to out-of-control marked with erratic behavior. Her death, at the young age of 36 is one of the first "mysterious celebrity deaths" in popular culture Marilyn Monroe was found dead of an overdose of sleeping pills on this date in 1962. Her life gives us a lot to think about in terms of what we consider to be priorities, the way we would like to live our lives and the legacy we would like to leave behind.

"I believe that everything happens for a reason. People change so that you can learn to let go, things go wrong so that you appreciate them when they're right, you believe lies so you eventually learn to trust no one but yourself, and sometimes good things fall apart so better things can fall together." — Marilyn Monroe

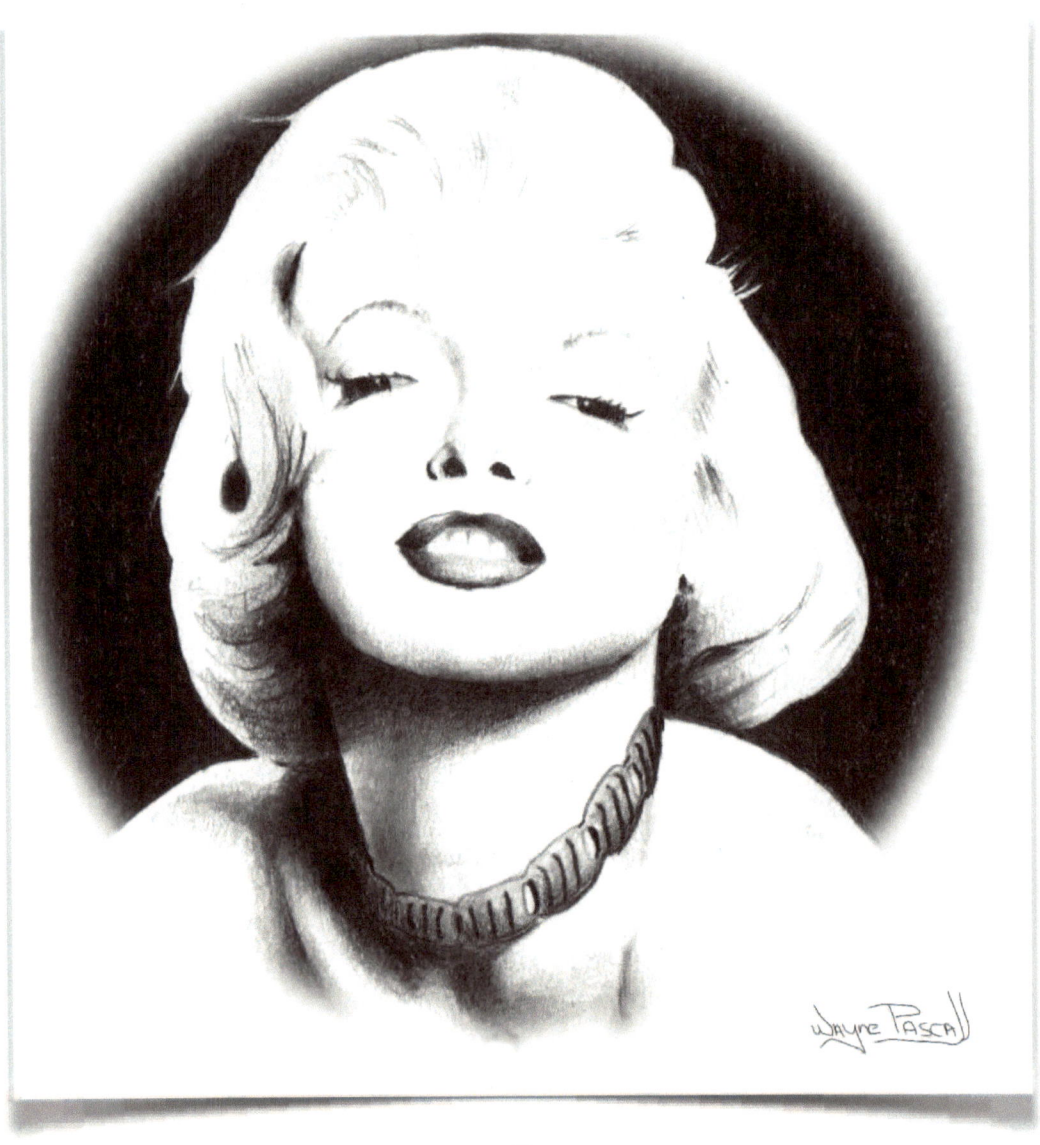

Marilyn Monroe

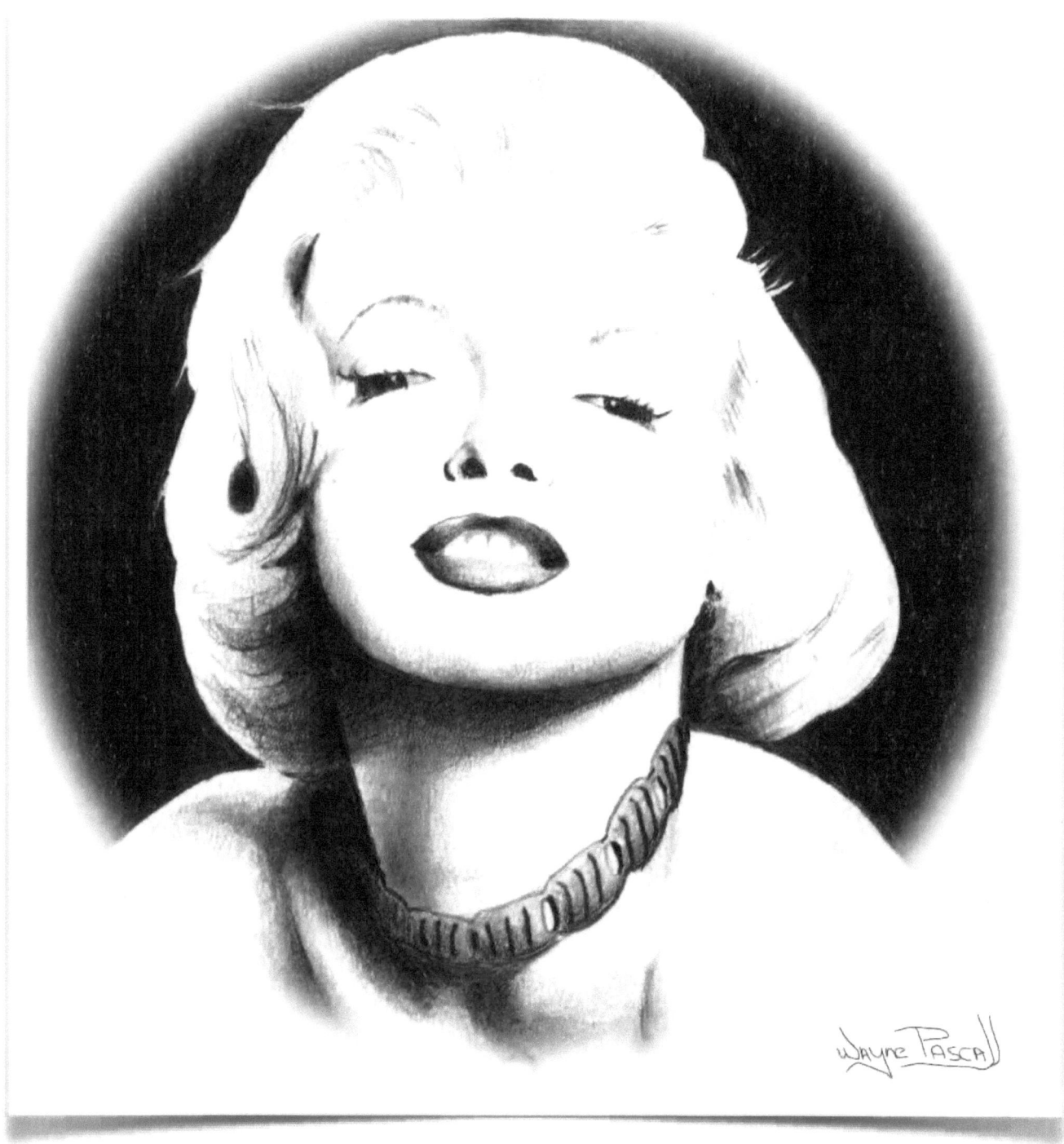

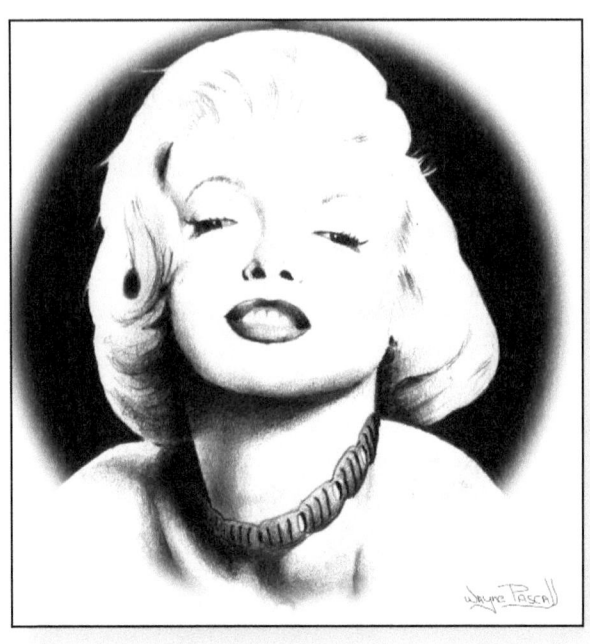

Marilyn
Wayne Pascall

http://wayne-pascall.artistwebsites.com/featured/marilyn-wayne-pascall.html

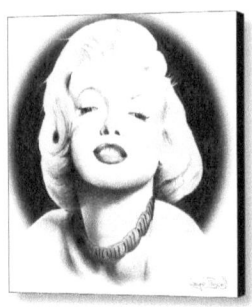
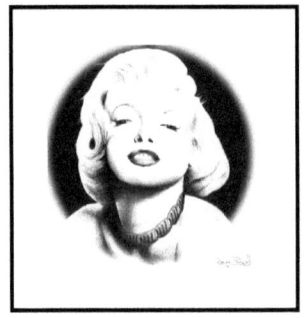
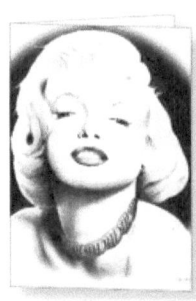

Stretched Canvases

Stretcher Bars: 1.50" x 1.50" or 0.625" x 0.625"
Wrap Style: Black, White, or Mirrored Image

7.75" x 8.00"	$47.04
9.75" x 10.00"	$65.96
11.63" x 12.00"	$82.86
15.63" x 16.00"	$110.48
19.50" x 20.00"	$136.47
23.38" x 24.00"	$172.54
29.13" x 30.00"	$227.46

Prices shown for 1.50" x 1.50" gallery-wrapped
prints with black sides.

Fine Art Prints

Choose From Thousands of Available
Frames, Mats, and Fine Art Papers

7.75" x 8.00"	$22.00
9.75" x 10.00"	$23.00
11.63" x 12.00"	$26.00
15.63" x 16.00"	$34.50
19.50" x 20.00"	$43.00
23.38" x 24.00"	$51.50
29.13" x 30.00"	$75.05

Prices shown for unframed / unmatted
prints on archival matte paper.

Greeting Cards

All Cards are 5" x 7" and Include
White Envelopes for Mailing and Gift Giving

Single Card	$4.95 / Card
Pack of 10	$2.70 / Card
Pack of 25	$2.00 / Card

Scan With Smartphone
to Buy Online

Ray Charles
RAY CHARLES (1930-2004)

Ray Charles was an American musician, singer-songwriter and band leader, born in Albany, Georgia on September 23, 1930. Charles became totally blind by the age of seven and never knew exactly why he lost his sight, There are sources that claim that his blindness was due to glaucoma, and others that Ray began loosing his eyesight from an untreated infection caused by soapy water to his eyes. He attended the Florida School for the Deaf and the Blind from 1937-1945, in St. Augustine, Florida where he developed and further enhanced his musical talent that he is known for today.

Ray's musical style was very varied ranging from rhythm and blues, rock and roll, soul, blues, pop, jazz and country all blended with a soulful gospel flavor. He helped to shape the sound of modern rhythm & blues. He brought a soulful sound to all genres of music he produced from rock and roll ("Mess Around") to country music ("I Can't Stop Loving You") to to pop rendition of "America The Beautiful."

"I can't stop loving you. I've made up my mind" — Ray Charles

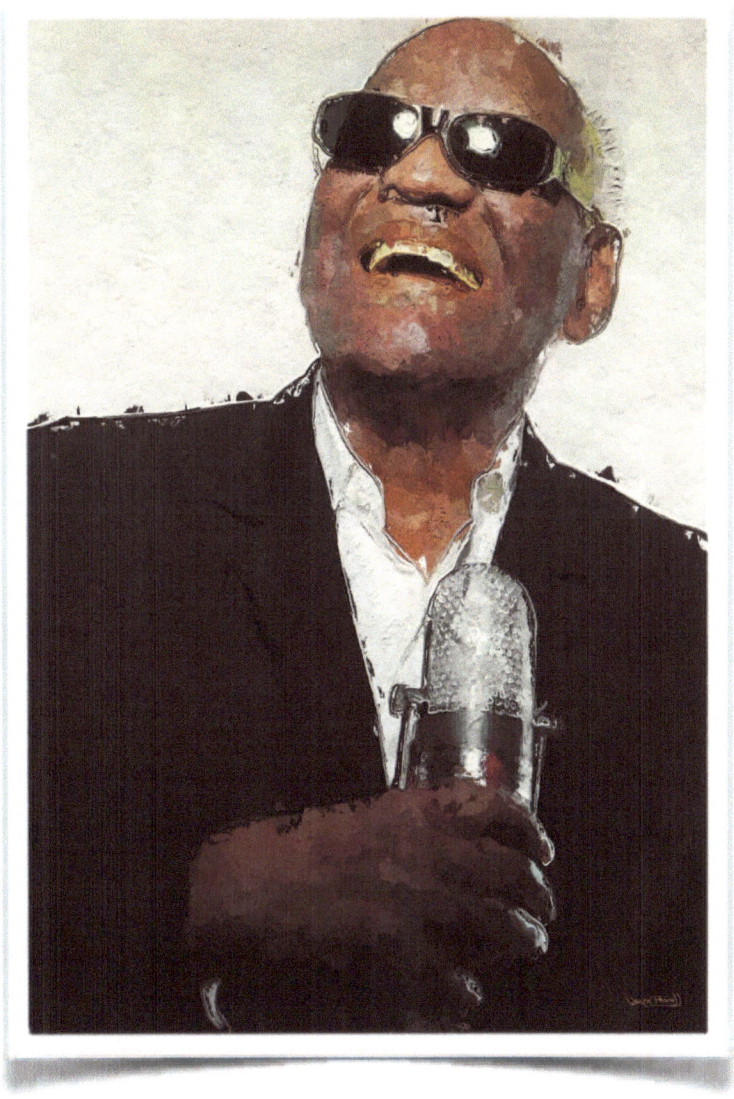

Ray Charles

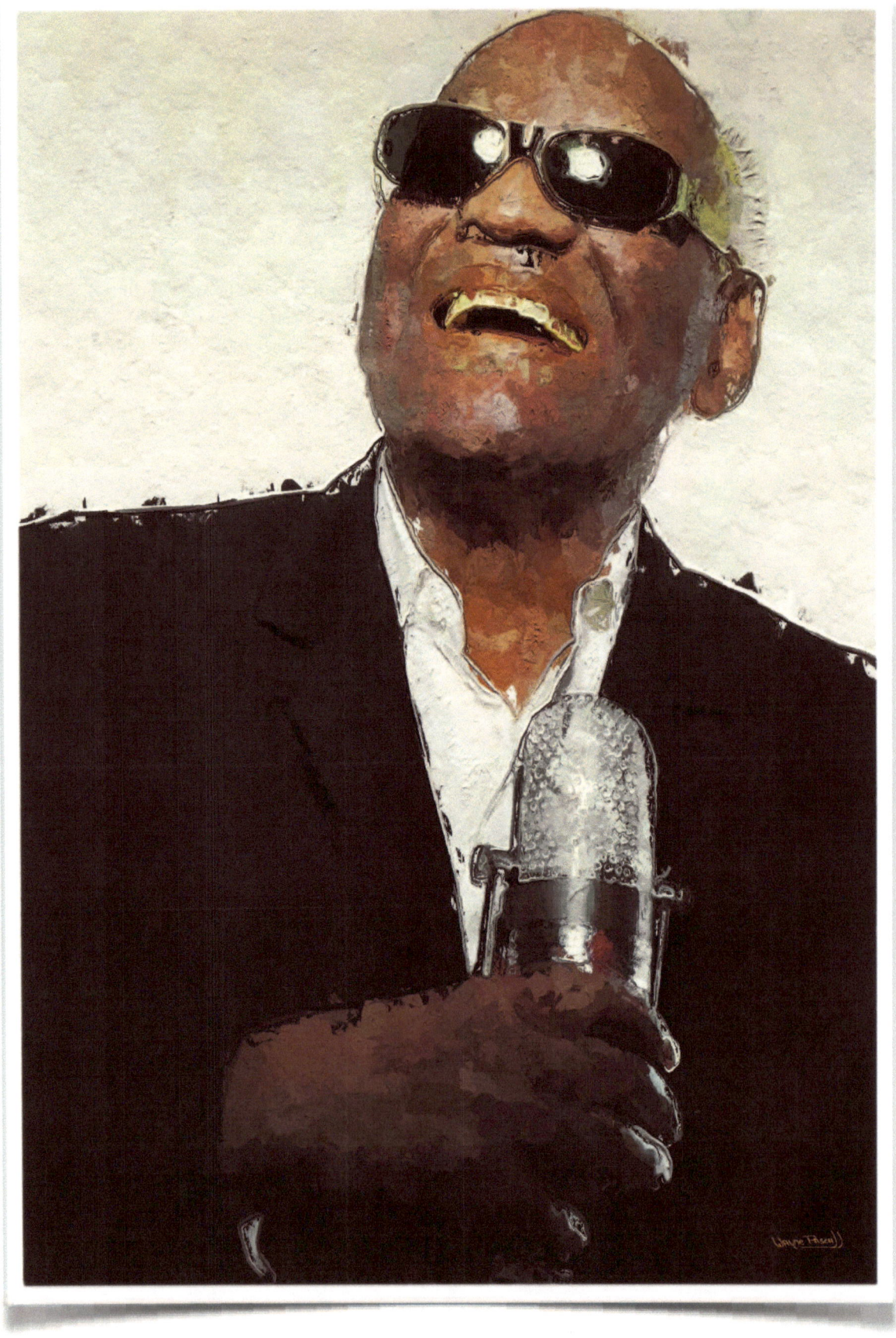

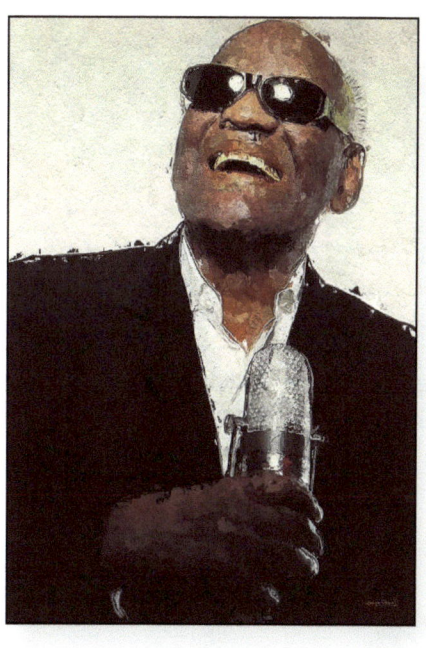

Ray Charles
Wayne Pascall

http://wayne-pascall.artistwebsites.com/featured/ray-charles-wayne-pascall.html

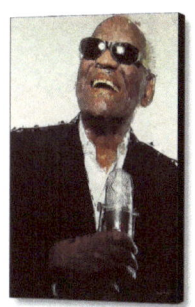
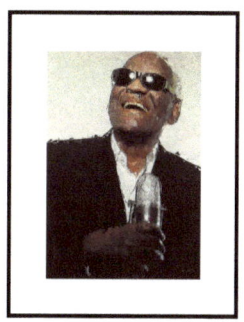
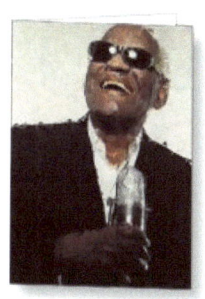

Stretched Canvases

Stretcher Bars: 1.50" x 1.50" or 0.625" x 0.625"
Wrap Style: Black, White, or Mirrored Image

6.88" x 10.00"	$74.96
8.38" x 12.00"	$84.96
9.75" x 14.00"	$108.86
11.13" x 16.00"	$137.17
13.88" x 20.00"	$204.98

Prices shown for 1.50" x 1.50" gallery-wrapped prints with black sides.

Fine Art Prints

Choose From Thousands of Available
Frames, Mats, and Fine Art Papers

5.50" x 8.00"	$27.00
6.88" x 10.00"	$32.00
8.38" x 12.00"	$42.00
9.75" x 14.00"	$52.00
11.13" x 16.00"	$70.50
13.88" x 20.00"	$129.00

Prices shown for unframed / unmatted prints on archival matte paper.

Greeting Cards

All Cards are 5" x 7" and Include
White Envelopes for Mailing and Gift Giving

Single Card	$4.45 / Card
Pack of 10	$2.30 / Card
Pack of 25	$1.60 / Card

Scan With Smartphone
to Buy Online

THE WOMAN AT THE WELL (ANNO DOMINI)

She was a woman with a promiscuous past of which she was not proud. Ostracized and despised by her pious society, she met a person by a well and one conversation with him changed her life. The person she met was Jesus The Christ as told in The Gospel of John chapter 4. She immediately became and ambassador for The Christ and went back to her village spreading the good news. Her life inspires us that it is never too late for a spiritual makeover, that at whatever point we are and whatever mess we have made in life, that the messiah can transform our mess into a message.

"Come see a man; who told me all things that I ever did: is not this the Christ?" — The Woman at The Well

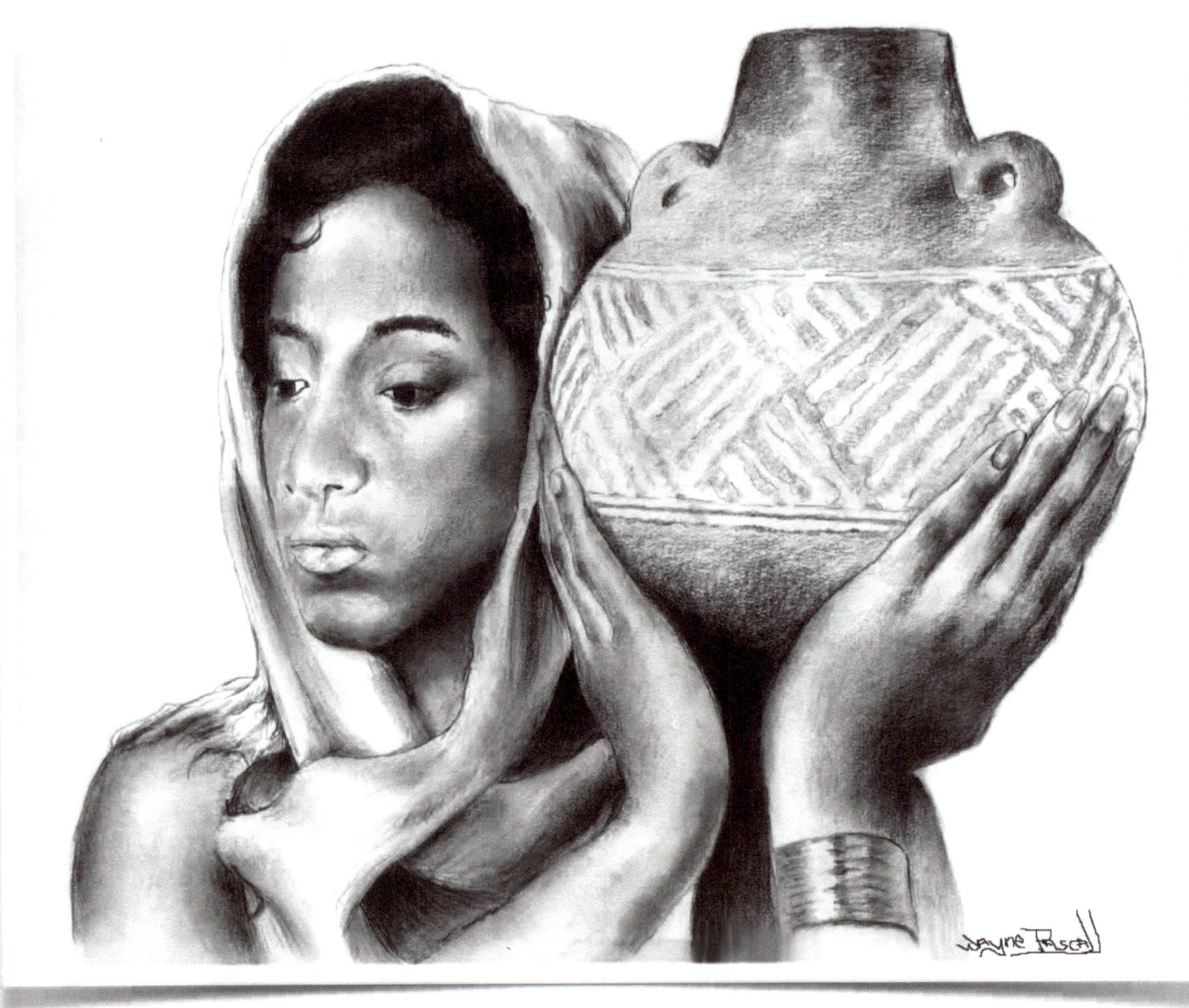

The Woman At The Well

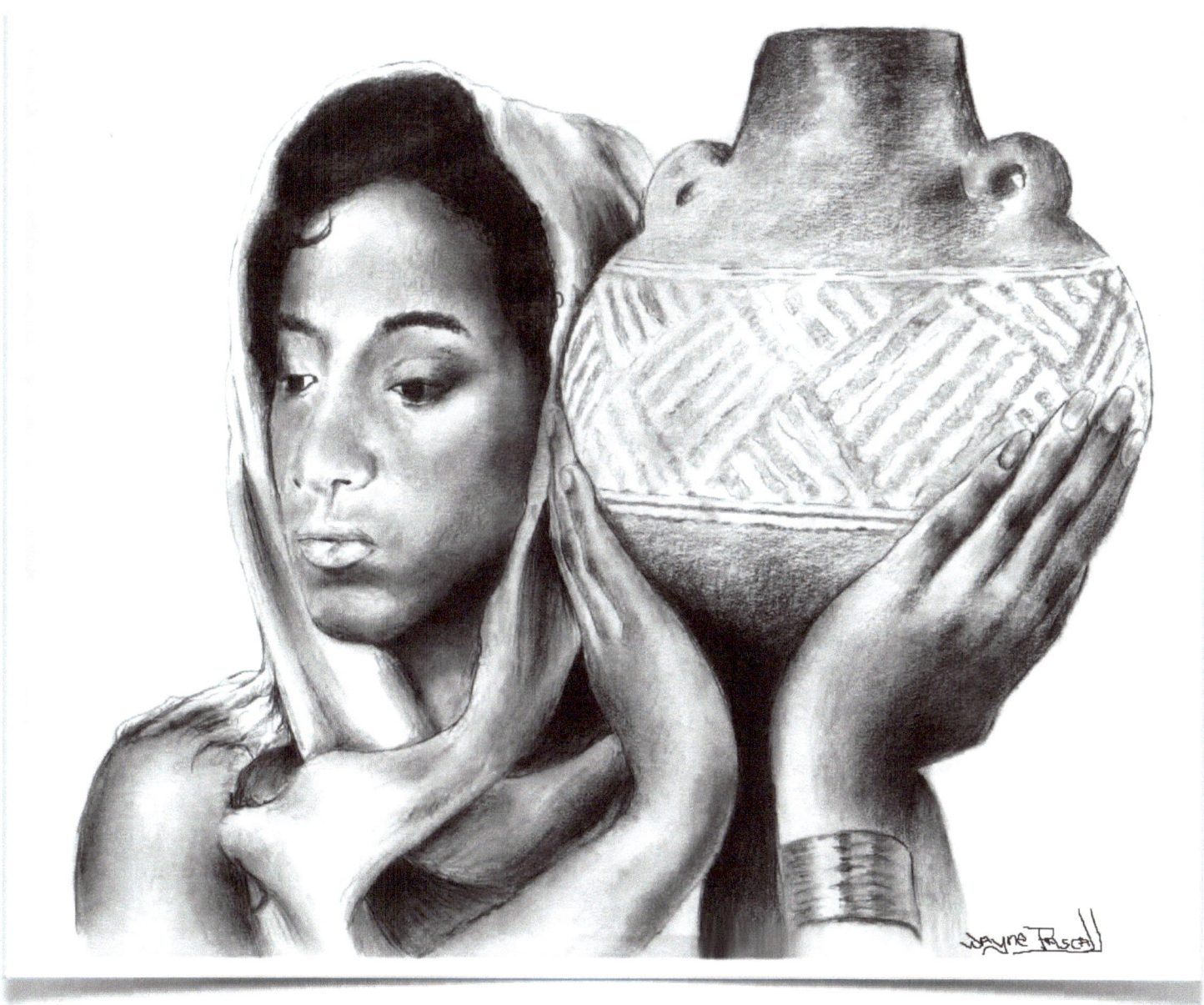

"Your work is going to fill a large part of your life, and the only way to be truly satisfied is to do what you believe is great work. And the only way to do great work is to love what you do. If you haven't found it yet, keep looking. Don't settle. As with all matters of the heart, you'll know when you find it." – Steve Jobs

"I'm enough of an artist to draw freely on my imagination. Imagination is more important than knowledge. Knowledge is limited; imagination encircles the world." – Albert Einstein

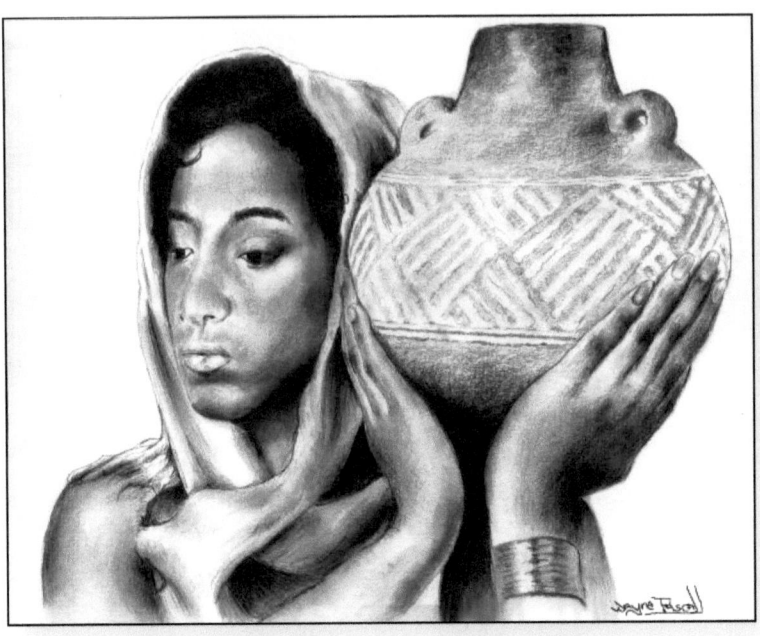

Water From the Well
Wayne Pascall

http://wayne-pascall.artistwebsites.com/featured/water-from-the-well-wayne-pascall.html

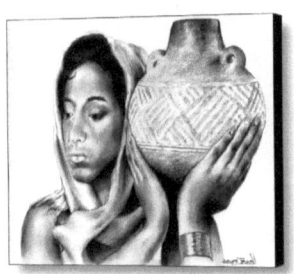

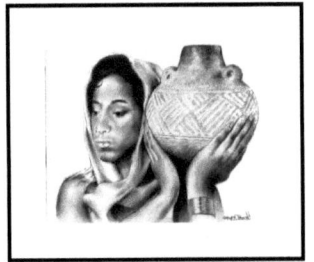

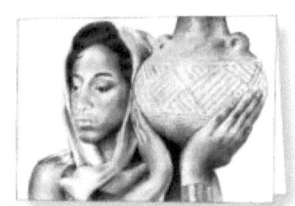

Stretched Canvases

Stretcher Bars: 1.50" x 1.50" or 0.625" x 0.625"
Wrap Style: Black, White, or Mirrored Image

8.00" x 6.25"	$47.04
10.00" x 7.88"	$65.96
12.00" x 9.50"	$68.96
16.00" x 12.63"	$97.67
20.00" x 15.75"	$124.41
24.00" x 18.88"	$149.76
30.00" x 23.63"	$206.62
36.00" x 28.38"	$249.20
40.00" x 31.50"	$289.65
48.00" x 37.75"	$373.28

Prices shown for 1.50" x 1.50" gallery-wrapped
prints with black sides.

Fine Art Prints

Choose From Thousands of Available
Frames, Mats, and Fine Art Papers

8.00" x 6.25"	$22.00
10.00" x 7.88"	$23.00
12.00" x 9.50"	$26.00
16.00" x 12.63"	$31.00
20.00" x 15.75"	$39.50
24.00" x 18.88"	$48.00
30.00" x 23.63"	$60.00
36.00" x 28.38"	$84.25
40.00" x 31.50"	$97.30
48.00" x 37.75"	$130.10

Prices shown for unframed / unmatted
prints on archival matte paper.

Greeting Cards

All Cards are 5" x 7" and Include
White Envelopes for Mailing and Gift Giving

Single Card	$4.95 / Card
Pack of 10	$6.95 / Card
Pack of 25	$9.50 / Card

Scan With Smartphone
to Buy Online

All prints and greeting cards are produced by Artist Websites (Artist Websites) and come with a 30-day money-back guarantee.
Orders may be placed online via credit card or PayPal. All orders ship within three business days from the AW production facility in North Carolina.